LEADERSHIP

Interdisciplinary
Reflections

Edited by
R. S. Khare
David Little

**UNIVERSITY
PRESS OF
AMERICA**

LANHAM • NEW YORK • LONDON

Library of Congress Cataloging in Publication Data
Main entry under title:

Leadership–interdisciplinary reflections.

    Proceedings of Birdwood Conference on Leadership,
convened March 1982 at the University of Virginia in
Charlottesville, Va., by the Committee on Comparative
Study of Individual and Society.
    1. Leadership–Congresses. 2. Interdisciplinary
approach to knowledge–Congresses. I. Khare, R. S.
(Ravindra S.) II. Little, David. III. Birdwood Conference
on Leadership (1982 : University of Virginia) IV.
Committee on Comparative Study of Individual and
Society.
HM141.L395   1984   303.3'4   84–7222
ISBN 0–8191–3969–6 (alk. paper)
ISBN 0–8191–3970–X (pbk. : alk. paper)

Co-published by arrangement with the
Center for Advanced Studies and
the Committee on Comparative Study of Individual and Society

TABLE OF CONTENTS

i

ACKNOWLEDGEMENTS

The Committee on Comparative Study of Individual and Society is grateful to the two guest speakers, Professors F. G. Bailey and Guenther Roth, and to the invited members from both within and outside the Committee listed as "Participants," for making the Birdwood Conference on leadership a rewarding experience. For the constant encouragement and financial support to organize the Conference and to publish these proceedings, the Committee owes a deep sense of gratitude to Dean W. D. Whitehead, Director, Center for Advanced Studies, University of Virginia.

During the preparation of the Proceedings, we received valuable help from the Committee's student assistants: Mr. Jean Jacques-Decoster, Ms. Laura Ushing, and Mr. Jeff Klein. Ms. Susan Owen offered us her thorough editorial expertise. This is to acknowledge their contribution with great appreciation.

R. S. Khare
David Little

PARTICIPANTS

Bailey, F. G.
Department of Anthropology
University of California -
    San Diego
La Jolla, CA

Bierstedt, Robert
Department of Sociology
547 Cabell Hall
University of Virginia
Charlottesville, VA   22903

Caplow, Theodore
Department of Sociology
542 Cabell Hall
University of Virginia
Charlottesville, VA   22903

Claude, Inis L. Jr.
Government and Foreign Affairs
207 Cabell Hall
University of Virginia
Charlottesville, VA   22903

Cohen, Ralph
Department of English
234 Wilson Hall
University of Virginia
Charlottesville, VA   22903

Crispell, Kenneth R.
Department of Medicine and Law
Towers Office Building 6200
University of Virginia
Charlottesville, VA   22903

Decoster, Jean-Jacques
Department of Anthropology
Brooks Hall
University of Virginia
Charlottesville, VA   22903

Feuer, Lewis
Department of Sociology
539 Cabell Hall
University of Virginia
Charlottesville, VA   22903

Hartt, Julian
Professor Emeritus
1939 Thomson Road
Charlottesville, VA   22903

Khare, R. S. (Chairman of
    Committee)
Department of Anthropology
303 Brooks Hall
University of Virginia
Charlottesville, VA   22903

Langbaum, Robert
Department of English
Wilson Hall
University of Virginia
Charlottesville, VA   22903

Little, David
Department of Religious Studies
B106 Cocke Hall
University of Virginia
Charlottesville, VA   22903

Roth, Guenther
Department of Anthropology
University of California -
    San Diego
La Jolla, CA

Shannon, David
Department of History
210 Randall Hall
University of Virginia
Charlottesville, VA   22903

Strong, Robert
Department of Government
and Foreign Affairs
Cabell Hall
University of Virginia
Charlottesville, VA 22903

Thompson, Kenneth
Government and Foreign
Affairs
232 Cabell Hall
University of Virginia
Charlottesville, VA 22903

Thorup, Oscar A. Jr.
Associate Dean, Medical
School
School of Medicine 1074
University of Virginia
Charlottesville, VA 22903

Whitehead, W. D.
Director
Center for Advanced Studies
444 Cabell Hall
University of Virginia
Charlottesville, VA 22903

Woodward, Calvin
School of Law
University of Virginia
Charlottesville, VA 22903

INTRODUCTION

A study of leaders and leadership may be best approached when it draws upon multidisciplinary scholarship. Convinced of this point, the Committee on the Comparative Study of Individual and Society convened the Birdwood Conference on Leadership in March 1982 (see Appendix). An attempt to discuss leadership in the modern world hardly needs justification. However, the foremost reason is that leaders and leadership continue to matter to different nation-states, developed and developing, for the matters of interdependence and joint survival. Whether good, bad or indifferent, leaders continue to affect critical human affairs, and an intrinsic interest in the subject must persist despite the fact that social science studies of "leadership" may not have been as promising as expected (e.g. see Paige 1977; and McCall and Lombardo 1978). The difficulty of the subject should demand more discussion, not less.

A conference such as this one had to set a modest goal -- a few general questions, reflecting the complexity that the topic carries in today's world. The conference also avoided to take any theoretical stance or favor a particular practical issue or condition. However, as indicated below, the main presentations and their discussions did fall into three interrelated conceptual themes and underscored a multidisciplinary perspective that was commensurate with the complexity of the topic. Leaders, heroes, and leadership -- all the three subjects were discussed during the conference.

The reasons for a careful approach to the subject of leadership are amply evident in the extant literature on the topic (for a comprehensive bibliography, see Paige 1977). Leadership has eluded any easy theoretical explanation, and the irrefutable generalizations are few. Though the earlier social science literature approached the subject of leadership with great enthusiasm and expectations, especially after World War II, the later researchers became increasingly cautious and careful. (For the earlier phase, see, for example, Weber 1957; Whitehead 1936; Gouldner 1950; Lasswell and Kaplan 1950; for the later phase, see Rustow 1970; Paige 1972, 1977; McClelland 1975; Winter 1973; and Lukes 1976). Leadership as a topic of study, began to draw upon wider sociocultural, historical, politicoeconomic, and philosophical factors. Thus, while dismay was writ large on some studies by the late seventies (e.g. McCall and Lombardo 1978), others took a decidely more descriptive, anecdotal, and humanistic turn (e.g. see Burns 1978, for a wide ranging survey).

In an overview, such a development could be interpreted in two divergent ways: it could either mean the disintegration of

1

leadership as a subject of traditional social science inquiry or a redefinition of a complex subject to suit the complex global concerns. The Birdwood Conference proceeded according to the second interpretation, and considered a multidisciplinary discussion both necessary and timely for the subject. The nature of the "crisis of leadership" in the late twentieth century was an important shared concern for most of the participants.

There were thus two basic reasons for the Birdwood Conference on leadership. First, the "crisis of leadership" in contemporary society raised a number of questions that interested the Committee members. For example, what is leadership? How is it produced and maintained in diverse societies and cultures? What are the contemporary crises in leadership? Do such crises exist in various cultures, or in just industrial societies? How do such crises get reflected in the critical issues of war and peace? By following the subject of leaders and followers in various cultures, these questions unavoidably involve the changing relationships between individuals and society in a comparative mode.

Second, leadership is a natural topic for a multidisciplinary committee that draws upon such fields of inquiry as anthropology, history, law, medicine, political science, religious studies, philosophy, and sociology. However, such a diversity has its advantages as well as disadvantages. Can such a diversity be coordinated to yield a coherent discussion of the subject? In there utility in trying? On the other hand, each of the above fields has a convergent and continuing stake in the study of leadership, and such a group's discussion, when conducted carefully, makes overlapping concerns evident.

The Conference was structured around three previously prepared presentations, an address by Kenneth Thompson, Director of the Burkett-Miller Center for the Study of Public Affairs at the University of Virginia, and two papers by guest participants. The Friday night opening address, "The Dilemmas of Leadership and the Modern (American) Presidency," was followed by a day long discussion of the papers by two guest speakers. The Saturday night session was given over to presentations by Robert Langbaum of the Department of English and Julian Hartt of the Department of Religious Studies, concerning the place of heroism for leadership in civilian politics and nuclear warfare as a challenge to contemporary political leadership. Finally, the last session on Sunday morning consisted of summary observations by the main speakers and some of the commentators.

The two principle speakers, drawn from outside the University of Virginia, were Guenther Roth, a sociologist of Weberian bent from the University of Washington, and F. G. Bailey, a British social anthropologist from the University of California, San Diego. Eight scholars from the Committee and the University were designated to respond to the two speakers.

Introduction

Robert Bierstedt and Lewis Feuer of the Department of Sociology, Calvin Woodard of the Virginia Law School* and Robert Strong of the Department of Government and Foreign Affairs commented in the morning upon Professor Roth's paper, "Our Responsibility Before History: Max Weber's Two Ethics and the Peace Movement." Ralph Cohen of the Department of English and Inis Claude of the Department of Government and Foreign Affairs, Theodore Caplow of the Department of Sociology and David Shannon of the Department of History commented in the afternoon session on Professor Bailey's paper, "Guardians and Princes: Strategies for the Control of an Entourage." After these comments, a general discussion followed.

Three interconnected issues involved in the study of leadership commanded major attention throughout the conference. They emerged primarily from the differences in outlook and interest represented by the two main speakers, Roth and Bailey.

First, there was the question of a micro- versus a macro-approach to the subject. True to the direction of his earlier work, Bailey is fascinated by the structure and dynamics of the relations of leaders to those closest to them "the entourage," as Bailey calls them. The focus is upon the techniques available to the leader for maintaining power by creating conditions of uncertainty and insecurity among those who surround the leader. Bailey's approach, thus, focuses intensively, and cross-culturally, on the strategies of social interaction between leaders and followers, whereas Roth inclines to take a broader historical perspective on the subject, especially in the context of Western experiences. He is interested, a la Weber, in viewing leadership via "ethical orientation." A leader, according to Roth, is part and parcel of a historical-cultural context. The leader is legitimated by and gives direction to certain cultural values. More generally, both Roth and Bailey emphasize that, without taking the broad cultural setting into account, together with the unique set of historically defined preferences and priorities, what is most significant about leadership will be missed.

It is presumably for this reason that Roth dwells in his paper upon the peculiar challenges to leadership in a contemporary industrial democracy like West Germany that are posed by the global threat of nuclear war. Roth appears to be suggesting that the phenomenon of modern political leadership cannot adequately be understood apart from the matrix of pressing international considerations (see Hartt also on the same topic).

The second issue follows from the first. It involves the question as to whether leadership is best studied by theoretical versus practical approach. That is, should the subject be approached in terms of certain sociological uniformities that are

---

*Note: Calvin Woodard's revised version of his comments could not be obtained in time for inclusion in the proceedings.

taken to be determinative of the phenomenon of leadership as such? This is Bailey's approach. A leader is a creation of social forces for Bailey. He is interested in studying the structure of social strategies between leaders and their associates and followers that are as typical, according to Bailey, of African chieftans as they are of American presidents or corporation heads. Consequently, Bailey proceeds as a social anthropologist, interested in the structure and meaning of comparative sociological regularities. In both his presentation and his remarks during discussion he emphasized general shared cultural and historical settings. Yet he did not lack a concern for the practical dimension since his concern for the general develops out of practical (even Machiavellian) strategies.

Comparatively, Roth's presentation characterized leadership, so to say, as a practical art, as the reflection and manipulation of practical values and interests that are very much conditioned by the historical and institutional context in which the leader operates. Roth seems less interested than Bailey in developing a 'comparative sociology of leadership.' Rather, his attention, as was Weber's, is devoted to the leader's 'ethical orientation' in his or her activity and self-understanding. For example, Roth gives an extended description in his paper of the rather complex interplay, in contemporary West German policy discussions, of Weber's famous categories, 'ethics of absolute ends,' and 'ethics of responsibility.' His major point is that the crisis of leadership in a contemporary Western democracy like West Germany is a crisis of moral assessment over nuclear deterrence and related policy questions. A central, if not the most important, thing to observe about leaders is, according to Roth, the way they respond to practical conflicts -- which is to say, conflict in values and policies -- that they confront in their social environment.

The third issue is, again, interrelated with the first two. It concerns the respective attitudes of Bailey and Roth to the place of public accountability and power in the study of leadership. For Bailey, leaders are most often involved in the subrational or nonrational manipulation of power to remain in power. Successful leaders have the capacity, as Bailey puts it, to give the impression of providing a public rationale for policies whose 'real reasons' are either left hidden, or are too manipulative or too incoherent to be publicly defensible. Although Bailey denies any 'Machiavellian' inspiration for his understanding of leadership, his sense of the 'strategic' and the 'practical' seem to betray such an affinity. Both Bailey's paper and his comments in the discussion tend to reflect such a likeness. At one point, Bailey even remarked that he does not much like leaders, just because of their eagerly indulged, if not unavoidable, need to rely upon deception and prevarication in the conduct of their affairs. But as he had observed at another point in the discussion, this exaggerated stance was itself a part of his strategy to encourage discussion.

Though Roth does not address the same issue directly, he seems inclined, as Weber was, to believe that leaders are both obliged and can, under proper conditions, be expected to justify their policies publicly. Such an expectation underlies, of course, Weber's whole notion of the 'ethics of responsibility,' which Roth makes so much of in his paper and his comments. It underlines, too, Roth's challenging suggestion that, under the threat of nuclear war, the 'most responsible' political leader may turn out to be the one who takes an unbending stand on further development and deployment of nuclear weapons. In any case, for Roth, there is no sufficient reason why leaders may not be held to public account.

The two presentations in the third session by Robert Langbaum and Julian Hartt added a humanistic viewpoint to the day's discussion. Langbaum's paper, "Shakespere's Ideas of Leadership in <u>Coriolanus</u>," raised philosophical questions of perennial concern. He asks us to ponder the question of Coriolanus' tragic end in the context of the Roman hero's un- yielding, if not monomaniacal, devotion to the preservation of his honor. At the conclusion of his paper, Langbaum asks whether a classical martial virtue like heroism renders Coriolanus an unfit model for leadership in civilian politics. Langbaum's discussion also underscores a more general question: What is the place of a hero, if any, in the late twentieth century society, and in national and international politics?

Julian Hartt's paper, "Apocalypse: The Ultimate Challenge to Leadership," relates directly to and extends Roth's considera- tion of leadership as a "political art" especially in the context of nuclear weapons and political leadership. Hartt asks whether it is either realistic or reasonable to expect political leaders to express a clear and powerful concern for the world-destructive potentiality of the nuclear arsenals of the great powers. Given the classical definition of politics as the art of the possible, are political leaders inescapably bound now to ponder the impossible possibility of humanity's extinction?

As expected, the above profile of discussion of leadership reflects both diverse concerns and differing stances taken at the Birdwood Conference. It reinforced the point that leadership is a socially complex and changing phenomenon, and a leader is not only a product of social contingencies and strategies but also a publicly accountable figure, a guide. Then, today's political leader also faces a deep and unprecedented crisis of values, especially as signified by the issue of nuclear arsenal and human survival. The significance of such a crisis is global; it concerns all nations and peoples, separately as well as together. This way certain issues of the first importance presented themselves to the Birdwood Conference for further discussion, bringing the study of leaders and leadership under critical, multidisciplinary focus.

Introduction

Given the diverse disciplines and their interests and perspectives, what was distinctly recognized during the Conference was the eagerness to learn from each other and to formulate one's own contributions for a wider, shared understanding. Though the Conference did not set out to resolve any particular issue, it did encourage the participants to develop multidisciplinary communications on critical issues. The impact of the discussions was substantive, for none of the participants will think about leadership the same way again.

R. S. Khare
David Little

BIBLIOGRAPHY

Burns, James M., 1978. Leadership, New York:Harper Colophon Books.

Gouldner, Alvin W. (ed.), 1950. Studies in Leadership, New York:Harper and Brothers.

Lasswell, Harold D. and Abraham Kaplan, 1950. Power and Society, New Haven: Yale University Press.

Lukes, Steven, 1976: Power: A Radical View, London:Macmillan Press.

McCall, Morgan, W., Jr., and M. M. Lombardo, (eds.), 1978. Leadership: Where Else Can We Go?, Durham:Duke University Press.

McClelland, David C., 1975: Power: The Inner Experience, New York: Irvington.

Paige, Glenn D. (ed.), 1972. Political Leadership, New York: Free Press.

Paige, Glenn D., 1977. The Scientific Study of Political Leadership, New York:Free Press.

Rustow, Dankwart A. (ed.), 1970. Philosophers and Kings: Studies in Leadership, New York:George Braziller.

Weber, Max, 1957. The Theory of Economic Organization, (ed. Talcott Parsons), Glencoe, ILL:Free Press.

Whitehead, A. N., 1936. Leadership in a Free Society, Cambridge:Harvard University Press.

Winter, D. G., 1973. The Power Motive, New York:Free Press.

SESSION ONE

THE DILEMMAS AND ANTINOMIES OF LEADERSHIP*
Kenneth W. Thompson

Whether the problem of leadership is related to the disappearance of heroes and hero worship from society is not altogether clear. The story is told of the senator who was returning from a Washington event and, recalling the people they had met, turned to his wife and said, "Isn't it tragic, darling, that there are so few great men left today?" And she turned to him and said, "There's one less than you think there is, darling."

Another perspective on leadership is the statement of a former colleague who said, when you get into the lion's den either the lion will get you or you will get the lion. The notion of confrontation illustrative of leadership on the attack. Another approach results from the transposition of phrases or words known to those of you who once had training in Fort Benning, Georgia. You may recall transposing the phrase which was a motto of shining new second lieutenants, "follow me," to read "follow you." It seemed a good deal safer under the circumstances.

I. Antinomies and Contradictions of Leadership

A more basic reason, however, that leadership is so complex and so difficult to assess and measure is that almost any

*A version of this appeared in Presidential Studies Quarterly, Vol. 14, No. 1, Winter 1984, pp. 35-42.

proposal regarding leadership presents a series of contradictions, tensions, and antimonies. Any proposition put forward from one standpoint about leadership is almost immediately subject to qualification on the other side of the ledger. Discussions of leadership become a matter of drawing a line down the middle of a page. In thinking about leadership, for every truth there is a balancing truth; in the application of leadership, for everything there is a season. What seems appropriate and effective in one era is less effective in another.

One quickly confronts such issues when he begins to think about some of the commonplace notions of leadership like the concept of the charismatic leader, the spiritual or political figure who captures the people's attention and imagination. In the state of Illinois where I lived for a decade, it was said that one of the great misfortunes for Governor Adlai Stevenson was that discussion never seemed to flow toward and center in him the way it did with charismatic and dynamic leaders. The mass of the people were not drawn to him. It wasn't that he didn't know as much or more than others nor was able to formulate and define issues clearly. But somehow the flow of discussion oftentimes went the other way. He was too reserved and too distant in personal relations. His associations were too formal and abstract. His demeanor ran counter to the image of a magnetic leader. He was lacking in the one area that some considered most essential for leadership. Another perspective in a leader is someone who is so average, so common and so mediocre as to appear the same as everyone else. This notion was voiced in connection with the nomination of a supreme court justice not so long ago defended in these terms. We were asked wouldn't you feel better with somebody who was as average as everybody else. In a more elegant and legitimate way Carl Schurz wrote regarding Lincoln as leader, "You are underrating the President ... I grant he lacks higher education and his manners are not in accord with European conceptions and the dignity of a chief magistrate. He is a well developed child of nature and is not skilled in polite phrases and prose. But he is a man of profound feelings, correct and firm principles and incorruptible honesty. His motives are unquestionable and he possesses to a remarkable degree the characteristic God-given trait of this people, sound common sense." In that one trait at least, Lincoln was seen as a child of the people.

In any event, the notion of inspiration and charisma is in tension with the notion of the leader as someone close to the people and not all that different from them. A similar tension exists between certain other elements of greatness. A former colleague at his death left an unpublished manuscript on Lincoln as leader. The first chapter is devoted to the greatness of Lincoln. Professor Hans J. Morganthau asks in his treatise what is greatness in any man and more particularly what is greatness in a statesman? He quotes Emerson on the uses of great men who wrote, "he is great who is what he is from nature and never reminds us of others."[1] He discusses uniqueness in the statesman and then goes on to compare it with uniqueness in other areas. Babe Ruth was a great baseball player, Pierpoint Morgan a great banker, etc. These men were great because they pushed one particular human faculty, whether physical prowess, culinary creativity or acquisition of money to the outer limits of human potentiality; they developed one human faculty to perfection. Then Hans Morgenthau comments, "But this is a limited greatness of a functional nature. A man is called great because he performs a particular function to perfection."[2] There is a difference between a great baseball player, a great chef, and so on and Emerson points to this difference when he writes of a great man that he must be related to us. Our life receives from him some promise of explanation. That is to say, a great man, in contrast to a man performing a particular function greatly, is one who at least approaches perfection in certain qualities of mind, character, and action that illuminate the very nature of man. He not only illuminates the nature of man but also holds up a mirror to his aspirations. He demonstrates in actual experience how far man can go and hence how much farther than he thought was possible a man can go who at least aspires to be great. "Great men," Emerson wrote, "speak to our wants."

Morgenthau goes on to argue that in these terms Lincoln appears indeed as a great man, of unique greatness combining within himself perfection of human potentialities to be found in such combination in few other men known to history. And he treats his statesmanship as greatness independent of success or failure. The unadorned qualities of his greatness have tended to disappear or at least become indistinct in the fact of mythological interpretations, but they persist in certain qualities which become the subject of Professor Morganthau's book and of his analysis.[3] Yet on the other side, effective leadership seems to involve something in which uniqueness, if it is present has to remain somehow credible. When I worked in New York one of the discussions in the early years of the Civil Rights movement was whether Ralph Bunche was in fact a leader for blacks and an example for other young aspiring minorities. The issue was whether Ralph Bunche was so far removed and so distant from the position of the ordinary black that in fact he gave them no leadership; looking at him gave them no example for their lives.

Further, in this general introductory profile of the main characteristics and major aspects of leadership, one should say something about the mystery of leadership. The person who said it best in his writings is Sir Harold Nicolson, especially in the Portrait of a Diplomatist which is an account of his father. Drawing on a portrait furnished by his daughter-in-law, he records that his father, Sir Arthur Nicolson, who was himself a diplomat, was: "Although physically so small and fragile, his manner was conceived upon a scale of ample but authoritative courtesy. He was impressive not insignificant. With all his gentleness, all his simplicity he contrived to impose his personality."[4] One is reminded of the pianist Arthur Rubenstein who was asked what is the first thing you do in a concert and he answered, "My first act must be to impose my presence upon the audience." Sir Arthur Nicolson in turn imposed his personality so that in a company of several people it was of his presence that one remained aware and to him that one naturally deferred. "He might sit silent in his arm chair watching, trying to hear, for he was growing deaf, but one could never forget that he was there. This quality must be due, one inevitably thought, to something essential in the man himself."[5] I used to wonder, Harold Nicholson wrote, what "is at the root of one's deference, respect and affection? For in spite of his irreproachable manners and his charm he is aloof, slightly unreal, removed from life by reason of his age, his disabilities and his absent-mindedness which come over him as he grows tired." But the answer was not hard to find. "It is not often," the son concluded, "that one meets a man whose absolute goodness and integrity proclaim themselves in the first glance of his eyes, as one first shakes hands, not often that one feels compelled to acknowledge the moral attributes as a basis of personal impression. Thus, however, it was with him. One's perception of him was most curiously and vividly compounded of physical compassion and spiritual homage."[6] Not surprisingly, Sir Harold Nicolson wrote these words in the language of the classics speaking of virtue, of goodness and of the good man. I remember talking well into the morning hours with Leo Strauss about his proposition that as you moved into any group you could somehow identify the person who had a kind of intrinsic or inherent goodness or virtue and that virtue might well have been a product of his self-fulfillment within the processes of social life and political life according to Strauss.

Yet this notion of the visible leader stands in tension with the notion of leadership which appears, although in different language and formulation in various discussions and papers. The leader is anti-leader; it is a characteristic of the leader that he conceals or downplays the fact he is leading. As an example, we are in the midst today of a revisionist trend of thought and writing about President Dwight D. Eisenhower and the "hidden hand" form of leadership which Eisenhower, according to Professor Fred Greenstein, practiced. He led but literally concealed his leadership from those who were trying to interpret his leadership. The example that comes most readily to mind is the McCarthy episode and Ike's refusal to speak out in support of General Marshall from a campaign train platform in Wisconsin. There is another anti-leader of course, a little bit less popular in some quarters, represented by Calvin Coolidge of whom it was said by Alice Roosevelt Longworth, that "the unsmiling Coolidge had been weaned on a pickle." Somebody else observed in the twenties that, "the American people wanted nothing done and Cal obliged them completely." And another observed in a more kindly vein that "he had no ideas but he was not a nuisance." This vision of leadership surely stand in contradistinction with the mystery of an all pervasive leadership.

II. Attributes of Leadership

If we go on to assess the most important attributes of leadership, the same tensions and antinomies are evident. What are some of the attributes of leadership in the political sphere, if one can enumerate them while leaving a more complete analysis to others? In political terms, one attribute is the role of the leader as unifier, harmonizer, and coalition builder. The Miller Center here in Charlottesville undertook a review of the presidential nominating process and invited testimony from former presidential candidates and their aides. A common bond that united George McGovern and the people who were responsible for the reforms of the nominating process in the late sixties and early seventies with conservatives on the far right was that they agreed that the nominating process as it presently exists virtually guarantees that a president would come to office without a coalition to govern. If you divest the nominating process of participation by those who possess the capacity which former Congresswoman Edith Green described as "having a sense of what is possible and practical," then you bring a leader to office without the mans of governing and without the capacity of pursuing his policies with the support of an effective political coalition. In fact, President Jimmy Carter's failure was largely a result of this lack.

So a President ought to be a leader, a harmonizer, a unifier and a coalition builder. But what about the situation where his task is to move the country ahead? What about the need for the President to be an antagonist as against the idea of his being a harmonizer? The person who, I suppose, best illustrated the role of antagonist was the old curmudgeon, Harold Ickes, who within the Roosevelt administration continually pressed and pushed, with very little help from others, for ideas which found their way into legislation. How do you resist special interests if your only task is to harmonize? Therefore, the two attributes of the leader as unifier and antagonist seem, at least provisionally, to be in tension.

Almost all government textbooks refer to political courage as the master virtue in politics, the ability to make decisions. A decision is something different from an opinion. A decision can't be put in a desk drawer and looked at a year or a day from now. People are required to stand up and make choices. But

13

how does the quality of decisiveness relate to the need we all feel for a normalizer particularly in certain circumstances? Walter Lippmann with all his preference for most of the ideas for which Adlai Stevenson stood, nevertheless came out in support of Dwight Eisenhower for President because he said Eisenhower could restore the country to a sense of normality and stability within its boundaries. He could restore people's self-confidence and satisfaction with themselves and their government. In that sense, lowering the temperature, slowing the pace at a certain moment in the cyclical movement of politics when the American people have grown weary and fatigued, either after a war or after a great leap forward in some social area, is considered essential. Gerald Ford after Watergate seemed to perform this function.

Another attribute of the leader is the attribute of judgment. I have a Charlottesville friend who describes her late husband as having a single dominant virtue and that was the virtue of judgment. She says others were brighter, more handsome, had more money; but her husband had judgment and the people of Charlottesville all knew it. This is not too far removed from what political theory teaches about leadership. Because acting in the context of politics puts a high premium on what an Indonesian friend, Soedjatmoko, has called sheer blind groping, judgment is vital.[7] In the making of political choice, the process is different from the process in which most of us engage most of the time as we seek for clarity in the intellectual, philosophical and scholarly area. Decision making involves the process of allowing facts, events and trends to wash over you, to listen for the rustle of the tide of events and then to grab hold of the garments of history as it moves past. It involves settling for some more or less harmful alternative in making a choice that has to be made. Thus judgment involves seeking for coherence and making the right choice. Those people who worked most closely with Harry S. Truman talked about his decisiveness, as the journalists did, but they talked about something else that in a way is even more significant. They said -- and these were intellectuals like Acheson and many others -- that he seemed to have all right instincts for the choices that had to be made. It was his instincts somehow, apart from pure rational deduction, that guided him to the right choice.

Yet if one carries this too far, if one reminds his wife when she wants to decide immediately on a matter to wait awhile and think twice about a decision, then the fact of Hamlet may be upon us. There is risk in the temptation to postpone decisions in order that one's judgment be improved. There are dangers in allowing history to overwhelm or pass over the decision maker. So the antinomy of the process of measured judgment, as I have described it, is the process of waiting too long. The historian, Walter Johnson, with all his faith and fervor regarding Adlai

Stevenson, nevertheless at the end of his biography comes down rather hard on Stevenson and his Hamlet-like quality. In defense of Stevenson, Johnson cites examples of the prison strike in Springfield when Stevenson was decisive and in command. Yet one almost senses in Johnson a protest that is too strong and too shrill.[8] Quincy Wright who taught at Chicago and Virginia never tired of telling a story regarding General Eisenhower. When Wright was an advisor at the Nuremberg trial, he needed money for some activity. He went to Eisenhower and said we can't go on with the consulting we are doing without money and he was sure that this would open up a long bureaucratic process. Eisenhower picked up the phone, reported Professor Wright, and announced that Wright and his colleagues needed such and such funds to carry on their work. As Wright walked out the door, somebody handed him an envelope containing the money.

Thus tensions exist between certain forces and one struggles to reconcile them. President Reagan has talked again and again about simplifying. He has said there is a tendency for intellectuals and those who write about policy to needlessly complicate problems which at root and with regard to essentials are basically simple. To the extent he has succeeded in certain policy areas, this quality of simplification is a strength for him in communication. However, there is a taint of anti-intellectualism in this view but also an element which within a democracy has some appeal. It was James Fallows who complained that President Carter was endlessly disposed to write every speech for the service station operator. H. L. Mencken once wrote "for every human problem there is a solution which is simple, comforting and wrong." These perspectives on politics have thrown the notion of simplifying into question. The trivialization and falsification of reality in politics seems to be the product of too much simplification. Television coverage based on a thirty-second or sixty-second encapsulation of the truth may leave one as far from the truth as one was before viewing the thirty-second capsule.

Another attribute of leadership involves conveying hope. Whatever anyone says in disparagment of President Reagan, he appears to have give some people hope. One reason the incumbent came to office, we're told, was because in contrast with Jimmy Carter he offered hope. But what about the other side. What about the Pollyannish depiction of reality when that reality has a major element of tragedy about it. Doesn't false hope contain inherent elements of failure? Don't ongoing problems require sacrifice? What about the disillusionment that follows the illusion which an effort at false or imaginary hope creates? The Norman Vincent Peale of politics is not always the leader with the most lasting impact. Yet the literature on politics by many political scientists has criticized politicians, including Mr. Carter, and politicians who are said to offer too little hope.

There are other attributes in politics, one being detachment, that are discussed in the substance of the manuscript on Lincoln from which I have quoted. Kennedy possessed a sense of detachment with his self-mockery. Lincoln perhaps had it at a more profound level with his objectivity. He had a capacity somehow, even in the midst of a Civil War to view the conflict as though he was looking at it from the other side of the battle lines as well as his own. He had the same objectivity and detachment with regard to himself and his personal appearance. He had it when he came to Washington after his election and was serenaded. What did he say to the serenaders? He responded, "I suppose I may take this as a compliment paid to me and as such please accept my thanks for it. I have reached the city of Washington under circumstances considerably differing from those under which any other man has reached it. I have reached it for the purpose of taking an official position amongst the people almost all of whom were opposed to me and are as yet opposed to me, as I suppose."[9] Imagine any other President who has just been elected in the face of a threatening rebellion on behalf of slavery coming into the District of Columbia where slavery is legal and finding himself serenaded by the supporters of slavery. Lincoln didn't try to gloss over the situation. He didn't offer any concessions nor did he ask for any from his audience. On the contrary, by defining the situation in all its unique starkness, he emphasized its absurdity. He looked at himself, he looked at the crowd and their mutual relations and not only recognized but also articulated his extraordinary position with objectivity saying, "I am alone, you are against me."

Consider the Civil War which saddled him with the crushing burden of enormous bloodletting, with long drawn out conflict, overwhelming the nation with all its international and domestic repercussions and all in good measure the result of the incompetence of some of the leaders, including the generals. On July 1st, Lincoln called for three hundred thousand volunteers using the phrase -- and can anyone imagine a present day leader using a similar phrase -- "so as to bring this unnecessary and injurious civil war to a speedy and satisfactory conclusion."[10] Imagine any President fighting a war, widely regarded to be unnecessary and injurious, calling for volunteers to fight it. Would he not appeal to the people to fight a necessary and beneficial war in order to obtain the maximum beneficial response? One can give even more telling examples of this spirit of detachment with regard to the interpretation of the struggle itself, the Civil War. This sympathy reflected itself in his attitudes towards deserters when he struggled with himself and with the law in trying in some more detached way to come to what he thought was an approximation of justice.

You may say, if this is the quality of leadership, what about enthusiasm for a cause? If detachment is a quality of leadership, what about the need for passion, what about the need for conviction and for taking a position which will inspire response by the people? Is there not an intrinsic tension between these two qualities which seem essential to success in politics? One writer has written of objectivity in observing a political situation that what is required of the statesman is to see clearly: first, to see his country and himself, then the situation of his rival, then that situation as his rival sees it, then his own situation as the enemy sees him. To see clearly means to see without passion, without the passion of pride, of hatred and of contempt. The statesmen must somehow master the paradox of wanting passionately to triumph over an enemy, to dominate that enemy to whom he feels passionately superior yet at the same time having to view his relations with that rival or enemy with the sense of detachment and objectivity which Lincoln attained.

III. The Tools and Constraints of Leadership

Let me treat two other issues briefly. One concerns the tools of the leader, the requirements of leadership. Top administrative officials who have served with a particular chief executive and been particularly close to him have stressed the role of the leader as sheepdog, the person within a democracy who rounds up followers who are more and more stubbornly resistant. My colleague, James S. Young, refers to the crisis of leadership as essentially the crisis of followership. The necessary ongoing, unremitting struggle to bring people on line through word and deed is an essential characteristic of leadership and of the requirements of leadership. Yet, other talks of leadership and of the requirements of leadership as involving the action of those who sound the clarion call. The leader is the trumpeter, the person who points the way. I'll come back to that.

How is one to fix these elements, these requirements of leadership in relationship to one another? In considering the tools and constraints of the leader, how is one to relate to the role of mastery of the last detail with commanding a grand design or comprehensive plan in order that those who are followers avoid a sense of drift and purpose? I once went to work for a man who had four different sized note pads alongside his desk, each larger than the other.[11] I thought this was the most unnecessary and ostentatious administrative action I had ever seen. But then I got to know him and I realized that each pad was there to note certain things that had to be done: big things or little things, inside things or outside things, dealing with junior colleagues or senior colleagues. I can't remember all the distinctions. But he used his administrative props and supports with great skill. He was stronger as a leader than many people with whom I worked because he succeeded in keeping the details in mind. It is appropriate to mention the Carter

17

White House oral history project conducted by the Miller Center. Several of the participants, particularly the young people who came to Washington with President Carter, have remarked about the enormous burden of the pressures of their work. Several of them have said, "Do you know that on certain days we get as many as twenty or thirty, even as many as fifty telephone calls. We never had that in other things we did."[12] Yet anyone who has had some degree of responsibility isn't for a moment surprised that one should get fifty telephone calls. The telephone calls simply chart the unending flow of demands and pressures by which one may be overwhelmed if one takes charge of events or if one lets them trouble and perplex he or she too much.

A friend from an earlier period who was second or third in command in the State Department had his secretary keep a stopwatch on him during a period of service. He wanted to learn how long he directed his attention to any given subject. The secretary found that the average time he gave during a working day to a single subject was two minutes. In a position where a succession of decisions are required, the flow of action, the flow of questions and requests, or little and big steps that have to be taken is so enormous that the person who thinks that he can master them all by working half time at the task is likely to be overwhelmed. However much we question the importance of being on the job and of working on details, one finds that something not attended to can lead to the breakdown of many, many good ideas. Woodrow Wilson was probably intellectually and morally superior to Lloyd George and Clemenceau in Paris measured by his vision, fervor and convictions. Yet Wilson cared not at all of the details of territorial settlements. He saw them as something that might be reached through cynical negotiations that lay outside the first duty of the President. However, those who had mastered the details at the Paris Peace Conference, who knew the historic background of states and regions and the demands of national groups were in a superior position in writing the treaty. Yet on the other hand, the person too immersed in detail, the person with no vision and no direction falls short of the man with vision. Hence the antinomy and the conflict. Winston Churchill asked at the beginning of one of his volumes why did we stumble into the First World War? Having looked at various reasons he answered his own question by saying "we had no plan." The West had no conception of what was required for achieving a concentration of power to resist power. We had no plan for using that power creatively and effectively through diplomacy. It is interesting that throughout his career Churchill constantly linked power and negotiations in a way that few statesmen have done. This was his grand design or plan if you will, something more than a collection of details.[13]

Another tension is the tension between private leadership, private diplomacy, executive privilege, and public responsibility.

This subject runs the gamut of almost every issue one is likely to explore including the settlement of disputes and the mediation of sharp differences. All of these issues obviously lend themselves best to some kind of private diplomacy and private settlement. But at the same time, many writers of note have called attention to the issue of accountability. On April 9, 1982, Admiral Rickover was a guest of the Miller Center.[14] He was somebody who throughout his military career made a religion out of accountability. He apparently would say to all of his subordinates, "I'm not going to judge what you do in this action or that action, but I'll judge you in terms of your accountability. I'm going to judge you as to whether you accomplish what you are asked to do and in accordance with the tasks you are called upon to carry out." Obviously, his idea was the notion writ large of public responsibility and accountability.

One or two final attributes involve the tension between ideas and to pervade discussions of leadership. Those people who were leaders seem to have been able to package answers to problems and seem to have had ideas about the management of such matters. They were more than mere technicians. They have a theory or philosophy. On the other hand, we have it from perhaps the most monetarily successful writer about his public service career, Henry Kissinger, that one doesn't get any new ideas once one takes on responsibility in the public service. One must live on the intellectual capital which he brings to the office.

How does one connect and relate all these issues? How does one measure them and what is one to think about the proposition regarding presidential leadership by someone who lays it down, though without any great certainty, that "it is the President who sets the tone, helps to shape moods and expectations and provides or fails to provide a framework for public understanding?" Of all the words that I have written, I think I have gotten more comment pro and con on that statement. On the one side, many of the presidential scholars say, "How do you expect a chief executive to set the tone, to help public understanding or to provide a framework? That isn't his responsibility." The task of the successful President is to be elected, to fashion a coalition and to institute a successful legislative program. But that wasn't what the Founders said. The Founders thought that it also was the task of the President to do certain other things. I suppose the question with which we begin in our discussion of leadership and predictably end is whether or not, in various spheres of leadership this function that I have just described is a necessary and realizable function of the leader.

NOTES

[1]Hans J. Morgenthau and David Hein, Essays on Lincoln's Faith and Politics, edited by Kenneth W. Thompson, (Washington, D. C.: University Press of America, 1983), 3-4.

[2]Ibid., 4.

[3]Ibid.

[4]Sir Harold Nicolson, Portrait of a Diplomatist, (Boston: Houghton Mifflin, 1930), 315-16.

[5]Ibid., 316.

[6]Ibid.

[7]Soedjatmoko is President of the United Nations University and his writings and speeches are regularly published in the publications of the University.

[8]Walter Johnson, How We Drafted Adlai Stevenson.

[9]Morgenthau, op. cit., 19-20.

[10]Ibid.

[11]The man was Dr. Joseph H. Willits, Director of Social Sciences at the Rockefeller Foundation who had been Dean of the Wharton School of Finance at the University of Pennsylvania.

[12]This attitude is recorded in an extensive oral history of the Carter White House based on the testimony of 70 administrators interviewed at the Miller Center.

[13]Kenneth W. Thompson, Winston S. Churchill: Statesmenship and Power (Baton Rouge, Louisiana: Louisiana State University Press, 1983).

[14]Kenneth W. Thompson, editor, The American Presidency: Principles and Problems, Volume II (Washington, D. C.: University of Press of America, 1983).

SESSION TWO

"OUR RESPONSIBILITY BEFORE HISTORY:" MAX WEBER'S TWO ETHICS AND THE PEACE MOVEMENT
Guenther Roth

I. Can Weber Help us Understand our own Time?

A hundred years after the death of Karl Marx, which will be commemorated the world over in March 1983, his secular theories about industrial society and his anarchic vision of the future have less and less to do with the actual course of events. But the same is also true of many of the anticipations of Emile Durkheim and Max Weber, who were still in their student years at the time of Marx's death. The three men had no inkling of the totalitarian horrors to come and could not imagine that within a few decades the technology and organization of industrial society would threaten all of life under both capitalism and socialism, either through sudden cataclysm or slow ecological deterioration. This is true even though Marx elaborated a theory of the self-destruction of capitalist society and Durkheim worried about anomic stresses in modern society. Weber considered it possible that the dynamics of industrial society could be arrested by bureaucratization ("Egyptianization") in the short run, and was certain that it would be stopped by declining energy resources in the long run.[1] But whatever evils Marx and Durkheim recognized in the society of their time, their optimism about the future of mankind was boundless, and this strikes us as utterly mistaken today. Yet Weber's sociological and political realism, too, which wanted to set itself off from both the faith in progress and the incipient fashion of cultural

21

pessimism, may no longer appear to us realistic enough. If Marx, Durkheim and Weber could not imagine the dangers threatening the world today, we should also concede that our own imagination cannot respond adequately to our knowledge of what can go wrong in the near future. Most social scientists see no possibility but to continue their own work as if nothing had changed in the world. Nevertheless, at least some of us should intensify our efforts to incorporate the secular changes of this century into theories of the course of social development and of the nature of modern society. There are, of course, good epistemological reasons for the belief that the gap between social theory and social praxis (or between structural history and the history of events) can never be narrowed satisfactorily. Our developmental and structural theories can only provide a basis for intellectual orientation and self-identification, for establishing where we seem to stand in the long perspective of history. In addition, for strategies of political action we need situational analyses, as they were attempted in varying degrees by Marx, Durkehim and Weber in their roles as political actors. Developmental schemes as such, whether of ideal or material developments, cannot provide guidance for action. Weber himself once pointed out that universal developmental tendencies -- he thought in particular of economic development -- cannot prescribe what a generation should do for the next: "A national leader will, of course, keep in mind those universal tendencies of development that will shape the external fate of the masses in the future. But as he is moved by the political destiny of his people, he considers the consequences of political changes for the next two or three generations, which will decide what will become of his people. If he acts differently, he is one of the literati and not a politician."[2]

Some recent investigations of Weber's writings have tried to clarify the levels of abstraction on which they operate.[3] I would like to suggest that his sociology now appears more clearly than previously acknowledged as a developmental history of western rationalism that cannot be applied directly to an analysis of our present troubles. It deals with great transformations over centuries. Weber's special sociologies of religion, law and domination -- the most elaborated part of his oeuvre -- provide a conceptualization for the study of long-range developments. His types of authority and administration are meant to promote broad historical comparisons as a preliminary to the causal analysis of major historical events. While Weber was greatly interested in the main historical modes of legitimation and administration, he was much less concerned with a theory of modern political leadership as a matter of statecraft or the arts of politics. When they appear at all in his scholarly writings, great historical figures, in particular the craftsmen of rulership, serve only as typological illustrations. There are, for instance, only a few passing references to charismatic leaders in contemporary politics, and the category does not even appear in the Collected Political Writings, with the exception of "Politics ad a Vocation," which stands halfway between the scholarly and the political writings.[4] The famous distinction between the ethic of responsibility and the ethic of conviction from the latter essay is a rudimentary sketch, not a systematic analysis.

What such an analysis must be like on the institutional and normative level has been shown by Wolfgang Schluchter, who has tried to formulate a theory, adequate for our time, of the mutual dependence of value-neutrality (or, more accurately, freedom from practical value judgment) in science and the ethic of responsibility in politics.[5] Rational politics is impossible without the information and clarification that only science can provide, and only a state committed to responsible (rational) politics will be willing to protect the institutional integrity of science. In responding to Jurgen Habermas' neo-evolutionary reconstruction of historical materialism, Schluchter has gone on to reconstruct in turn Weber's stages of ethical development; the ethics of conviction and responsibility are not just juxtaposed, as Weber himself tends to do, but put into a historical sequence. The ethic of conviction is superseded by a reflexive ethic of responsibility, which must be our own yardstick insofar as we commit ourselves to rational science and rational politics.[6] This is significant updating and upgrading of Weber's developmental perspective, but it must remain a formal solution; it cannot be a guide to practical decision making. For the latter, we must turn to Weber's political writings.

In his political writings Weber offered a national agenda for the conduct of German "world politics." This involved the evaluation of the power distribution among contending groups and the formulation of diplomatic and constitutional solutions. Weber drew on the arsenal of his historical typologies and secular theories, but persuasion, not detached analysis, was his goal. He tried to persuade with his analytical skills and the depth of his historical knowledge, and he did not hesitate to use the distinction between the two ethics for his own political purposes. Just as we cannot expect to find Weber's sociology to be directly helpful for understanding our own political situation, so we must not expect his time-bound political writings to be directly applicable to our time. It so happens, however, that his two ethics have become part of German public discourse on the nuclear arms race and the NATO defense policies at the same time that the background of the distinction between the ethics has been forgotten. Therefore, I propose to look at the two ethics in the context of Weber's political agenda, especially his notion of "our responsibility before history," and at the adequacy of their present-day uses. Thus, I would like to identify one possible historical framework for understanding the present situation.

2. Troubles and Rhetoric in the Atlantic Alliance

The political relations between the United States and West Germany are today worse than they have been since their co-operation began in the late 1940's. With the advent of the Reagan administration the American policy of massive (re)arma-ment and global strategy of confronting left-wing movements everywhere coincided with the severe world recession and the rise of vociferous large peace movement in Europe, which was later followed by an American counterpart. In West Germany the economic crisis undermined the prestige and stability of the coalition government of SPD and FDP at the same time that a strong left emerged in both parties. In addition, the European peace movement, which is not wholly identical with the left, found a particularly enthusiastic response in West Germany. At the center of the controversy lay the NATO double resolution (or two-track decision) of 1979, which proposed a classical balance of power ploy (part of "responsible" politics): either the Soviet Union would agree to withdraw or dismantle a signi-ficant number of its intermediate-range missiles targeted at western Europe or Pershing II and cruise missiles would be installed at the end of 1983, escalating the nuclear armament spiral by several rotations. The NATO double resolution was promoted by Chancellor Helmust Schmidt before it became clear to him that its implementation would have to be attempted in the face of the worst postwar economic crisis and a growing peace movement. The Polish coup of December 1981 exacerbated the difficulties for Schmidt's efforts to mediate between Reagan and Breshnev. In the winter of 1981 Schmidt, who used to have a good international press, was suddenly attacked not only by American but also by British and French mass media for lack of a "principled" policy, whereas inside West Germany he was already accused by the peace movement of being an irresponsible champion of the balance of terror. To the American government Western Europe and especially the Federal Republic seemed to be pursuing narrow economic interests, particularly the natural gas deal with the Soviet Union, and the peace movement looked like a danger to peace. Conversely, President Reagan appeared to many Europeans as the first ideologist in the White House since Woodrow Wilson. In this situation Weber's two ethics resurfaced in the German discourse about foreign policy. Their logic un-derlay the controversies not only implicitly but at times expli-citly, as in exchanges between Chancellor Schmidt and some of his opponents. The media too helped to direct attention to the two ethics. For instance, in response to the domestic and foreign criticism of Schmidt the leading German weekly, the liberal "Die Zeit," published a full-page excerpt from "Politics as a Vocation" in its issue of January 8, 1982. The journal claimed that Weber's famous speech of 1919 has lost little of its relevance and that every self-respecting journalist could recite the maxim: "Politics means a strenuous slow drilling of hard boards." In the same journal, on January 29, the redoubtable Countess Donhoff, perhaps the most respected editorialist in West Germany, compared the public reactions of President Reagan and Chancellor Schmidt to the Polish developments in terms of the two ethics: "The principled political leader reacts to violations of human rights as automatically as the fire truck to an emergency call. The responsible leader must examine the means, consider the principle of proportionality and keep in mind the likely outcome of a course of events. We cannot say that one attitude is more moral than the other, for the principled leader, who proudly points to his white vest, can cause more damage than the responsible leader who risks the odium of acting morally but in an indirect way. In politics, at any rate, a measure of pragmatism is unavoidable. But this does not mean that we can act without moral standards. Politics without morality leads to opportunism and cynicism and to the disintegration of state and society." After this typological juxtaposition, she pointed out that "in the case of Poland President Reagan reacted very vociferously. He told us that he had to restrain himself not to call for a Polish uprising. This statement shows that he is capable of much sympathy and of little political understanding."[7]

If we disregard the political rhetoric, which of course has serious consequences of its own, we can see that in their choice of actual countermeasures all western governments have been quite cautious. It may have been too simple to identify Schmidt's diplomatic balancing act as an ethic of responsibility and Reagan's rhetoric as expressive of an ethic of conviction, rather than of frustration or a tactical response to voters of Polish descent. In the meantime we have seen that no amount of calculation of consequences has improved noticeably the chances of success for an effective western policy in the Polish case.

In general, in every critical situation political combatants are likely to accuse one another of "lack of principle" and "irresponsibility" and to find the qualities of leadership listed in Weber's "Politics as a Vocation" wanting in the adversary; and they are likely to feel that their opponents lack of the patience and stamina required for that "strenuous slow drilling of hard boards." Let us see, therefore, whether the revival of the two ethics in German public discourse involves more than reversible rhetoric, whether consistent political positions can be identified or whether indeed a new historical situation has arisen that makes it more difficult than ever before to decide who follows one or the other ethic. First, however, we must take a closer look at Weber's own understanding of the two ethics, especially in relation to his notion of "our responsibility before history" in his political writings.

3. "Our Responsibility Before History:" The Political Context of Weber's Ethics in Imperial Germany

The term "ethic of conviction" (or of single-minded com-mitment, conscience, good intentions or ultimate ends) -- there is no satisfactory translation of Gesinnungsethik -- first ap-pears, mostly as an adjective, in Weber's studies in the economic ethics of the world religions and the related chapter on religion in Economy and Society. Like charisma, the term has a religious origin. It refers to conduct based on the purity of faith rather than on obedience to the injunctions of religious law (law ethic). In the political realm, two social types represent the ethic of single-minded commitment, the revolutionary and the pacifist. In contrast to the ethic of conviction, the phrase "ethic of respon-sibility" was coined only in "Politics as a Vocation," but the underlying idea was already present in Weber's earliest political writings. It is a specifically political category. In the very sketchy outline for his speech Weber replaced "power politics" with "the politics of responsibility." He needed a term to set himself off from the worship of Realpolitik among his political opponents on the right, whom he berated for their political irresponsibility and stupidity. By choosing the term "policy (or ethic) of responsibility" he could emphasize the ethical element in politics and better confront not only the amoral political right but also the political left with its genuine or pretended good intentions.

"Politics as a Vocation" was delivered in Munich in early 1919 before a political student group which had run for some time a series of off-campus lectures on the professions. But it was a bad time for detached vocational advice. Munich was in the throes of civil war. Weber and his listeners were faced with overwhelming uncertainties. He had lost more than his younger listeners had: his twenty-five year long struggle for a national policy under the motto of "our responsibility before history." In view of the purpose of the lecture series Weber was justified in taking a pedagogical rather than political stance. He knew that his audience might expect a political speech from him -- he gave many at the time. Therefore, he warned his listeners imme-diately that he would address "actual problems of the day... only in a purely formal way and toward the end when I shall raise certain questions concerning the significance of political action within our conduct as a whole."[8] Two-thirds of what he chose to say was sociological in the sense that he presented a sketch of the developmental history of the modern state and a typology of political agents and functionaries. Only the last third dealt with the ethos of politics. Weber tried to contrast the two ethics "in a purely formal way," but he did not really succeed, and perhaps did not seriously intend to be merely formal. It appears to me that the formal emphasis of his exposition was less the fruit of a long process of reflection on the two ethics, but has more to do with the crisis of Weber's own substantive policy or ethic of responsibility. He himself was adrift and searching for a new political position in quickly shifting situations. For decades he had bitterly attacked the Imperial and Prussian government and the political right from the viewpoint of his "policy of responsibility." They had just collapsed for internal and external reasons, and his political opponents on the left were moving into the power vacuum. It is not surprising, therefore, that Weber now singled out the left, whether pacifist or militant, and that his speech turned, after all, into a political warning.[9] He warned of merely "noble intentions" that do not face up to the facts of power and declared that "the Bolshevik and the Spartacist ideologists bring about exactly the same result as any militaristic dictator.... In what but the persons of the power-holders and their dillettantism does the rule of the workers' and soldiers' councils differ from the rule of any power-holder of the old regime?"[10]

Whereas Weber pointed to the revolutionaries' difficulties to avoid falling back into their opponents' routines for power, he tended to press the pacifists for a total consistency that was beyond normal human capacity. In "Between Two Laws" (1916), which deals with the two ethics without yet naming them, he pleaded not only for an understanding of "the tragedy inherent in the historical duties of a people organized as a power state," but also identified the web of guilt in our daily lives, which made the consistency of an ethic of conviction very hard to attain even for pacifist virtuosi: "Whoever takes only one penny of interest from others, directly or indirectly, whoever owns or uses a commodity produced with another person's sweat, lives off the machinery of that loveless and pitiless economic struggle for existence which the bourgeois ideologists like to call 'peaceful civilization'.... Whoever does not face the consequences -- and Tolstoy did so only under the shadow of death -- should be reminded that he is tied to the rules of this world, and that includes for an unforseeably long time the possibility and inevitability of war. Only under these constraints can he satisfy the 'demands of the day.'"[11]

If revolutionaries and pacifists can live up to the ethic of conviction only with great difficulties, what about the adherents of an ethic of responsibility? Presumably they must beware of pursuing mere power politics, but Weber does not identify them as a group. We have no trouble recognizing the political targets whom he labels as adherents of an ethic of conviction, but he leaves us with only abstract features of "responsible" action. What are we to make of the famous observation that "politics means a strenuous slow drilling of hard boards, requiring passion and a sense of proportion?" In 1896 Weber had been more concrete: "Politics is a strenuous exercise (hartes Geschaft), and whoever wants to take upon himself the responsibility for

27

grasping the spokes of the steering wheel that guides the development of the fatherland must have good nerves and must not be so sentimental that he cannot conduct a down-to-earth policy."[12] Apparently, before his listeners in 1919 he felt that he could no longer repeat his old appeals, referring illustratively to "the future of socialism or international peace" instead of "the fatherland, which at present may be a dubious value to some."[13]

Weber had entered the political stage as a self-conscious generational spokesman in the early 1890's. He asked his generation to take responsibility for the next through the pursuit of a globally-oriented policy. Under Bismarck's leadership, his father's generation had brought about Germany's unification. Weber felt the "grave curse" of belonging to an epigonic generation, but he wanted to overcome this sense by having his generation shoulder the responsibility for a grand German "world policy."[14] In his notorious inaugual address at the University of Freiburg in 1895 the remarkably young full professor of economics staked out his generational claim.

> If we think beyond our own graves, we are not concerned with how well off people will be in the future, but what kind of people they will be.... We want to impart to them not hedonistic well-being but those qualities we believe account for human greatness and the nobility of human nature.... Our descendants will hold us responsible before history, not primarily for the economic organization we hand on, but for the elbow room we achieve and leave for them in the world.... We must understand that the unification of Germany was a youthful prank which the nation perpetrated in its old age and which it would better have avoided in view of its costliness, unless it was intended to be not the end but the beginning of a policy of German world power.

Therefore, Weber concluded: "Even in the face of the terrible misery of the masses, which weighs heavily on the sensitized conscience of the new generation, we must honestly profess that more burdensome is the awareness of our responsibility before history."[15]

In his Frieburg address Weber wanted to challenge, among others, the international "ethical culture" movement, but at other occasions he railed no less against the "empty zoological nationalism" rampant among the students.[16] In his struggle against both sides the core of his own ethical rigorism was that very "responsibility before history" which he admitted was a "somewhat pathetic" notion (that means, laden with pathos).[17] This ethical rigorism was linked early with a theory of imperialism. Weber expected increasingly violent struggles among the "civilized bourgeois nations" (Kulturvolker) and therefore supported the naval expansion in 1898: We must "make continuous military sacrifices in the interest of our future for which we, as a great nation, are historically responsible to our descendants."[18]

From the very beginning, however, Weber's advocacy of a policy of responsibility had a double aspect, which became increasingly important the more he felt himself forced into an outsider role and into "critique as a vocation."[19] Positively, Weber's advocacy involved the notion of a German world policy; negatively, it warned of the totally inadequate and self-defeating ways in which this policy was pursued. It was only consistent that during the First World War Weber emerged as one of the most vociferous critics of the conduct of the war and of the annexationist aims of the right. But he also tried to defend Germany's role by expanding the theme of historical responsibility, which now appeared no longer merely a matter of creating more elbow room for one's own country on the capitalist world market. In February 1916 he replied to an article by a Swiss pacifist woman that "our responsibility before history" also involved the welfare and integrity of the smaller countries of Europe. A great power such as Germany has tasks different from those of the smaller countries, although this implies no cultural superiority. In fact, smaller countries can more easily devote themselves to the pursuit of cultural values (Kulturguter), from civic virtues and democratic habits to literary achievements. Justifying the German war cause in terms of honor (rather than annexations) and of cultural responsibility, Weber argued that it was also in the interest of the smaller countries that the world not be divided "between the rules and regulations of Russian bureaucrats and the conventions of Anglo-Saxon 'society,' perhaps with a dash of Latin 'raison'.... Because we are a great power (Machtstaat) and, unlike the 'small' countries, can throw our weight into the balance on this socre, we have the damned duty before history, that means, before posterity to oppose the flooding of the whole world by these two powers." Repeating his theme from 1895 about the meaning of German unification, he added: "If we refuse this obligation, then the German empire is a costly and vain luxury, detrimental to culture, in which we should not have indulged and which we should abandon as soon as possible in favor of the 'Swissification' of our state."[20]

A few months later Weber repeated his view of Germany's responsibility toward smaller countries in a speech in Munich (October 27, 1916), the publication of which was censured: "Posterity will not hold responsible the Swiss, the Danes, the Dutch, the Norwegians for the cultural development of the world. It would not blame them if in the western hemisphere nothing were left but Anglo-Saxon convention and Russian bureaucracy. And rightly so. Because the Swiss or Dutch or Danes cannot prevent it. But we can.... It has been our fate to be a people of seventy millions and not of seven. This is the basis for that inescapable responsibility before history which we could not avoid even if we wanted to. We must make this clear time and again, if today the question about the 'meaning' of this endless war is asked."[21]

Weber's own cultural commitment was to a morally autonomous individualism, a liberal Protestant idea reinforced by Kantianism. It is striking, however, that his vague plea for keeping the cultural options of the future open in the name of western pluralism was not followed up by any positive statement of the specific German contribution. In fact, Weber took a very dim view of it, energetically criticizing "the German ideas of 1914" and similar claims to German cultural superiority. In elaborating his proposals for constitutional and electoral reform (in December 1917), he openly admitted that the trouble lay with the dismal nature of German political culture, which did not measure up to the democratic dynamics of the Anglo-Saxon and Latin conventions: "For despite the occasional boasting of our literati, it is completely untrue that individualism exists in Germany in the sense of freedom from conventions, in contrast to the conventions of the Anglo-Saxon gentleman or of the Latin salon type of man. Nowhere are there more rigid and compelling conventions than those of the German 'fraternity man'.... From a political point of view, it is still more important that, in contrast to the Latin and Anglo-Saxon countries, these German forms are simply not suited to serve as a model for the whole nation down to the lowest strata.... The Latin code of honor, as well as the quite different Anglo-Saxon code, has been suitable for far-reaching democratization."[22]

Weber's advocacy of parliamentary government within the monarchic framework seemed to come to fruition in October 1918, when Prince Max von Baden became chancellor, with whose political advisers Weber had close ties. But within days Imperial Germany collapsed and with it the chance for a stable peace settlement. On October 27 Weber made a hopeless appeal to his colleague-in-politics, Woodrow Wilson, in an unsigned editorial in the "Frankfurter Zeitung," defending for the last time the need for a balance in world politics.

> Men of good will and understanding do not question President Wilson's sincerity. It appears, however, that he does not sufficiently grasp the following: If the German government accepts his armistice conditions, which make any further military resistance impossible, not only Germany but he too would be eliminated as a major factor in the peace settlement.[23]

There was no realistic possibility for such considerations to play a role in Wilson's mind, and both men were to suffer unmitigated failure because of the outcome of the Versailles treaty. Weber's political world collapsed first: in a letter of November 24, 1918, he conceded the end of his political vision of Germany's responsibility before history and referred to the new position of the Anglo-Saxon countries and of Russia: "The self-discipline of truthfulness bids us to say that Germany's role in world politics is over: Anglo-Saxon world rule ... is a fact. It is more disagreeable, but we have averted far worse things -- the Russian knout! No one can take that glory away from us. America's world rule was as inevitable as that of Rome after the Punic Wars in ancient times. I hope it will continue not to be shared with Russia. To me that is the goal of our future global policy, for the Russian danger has been averted only for now, not forever."[24]

It is not surprising that in the same letter the author of "The Protestant Sects and the Spirit of Capitalism" should advocate as a means of moral regeneration an element of those very Anglo-Saxon conventions of which he had warned during the war: "Foremost among [our cultural tasks] is the restoration of that prosaic moral 'decency' which, on the whole, we had and which we lost in the war -- our most grievous loss. Massive problems of education, then. The method: only the American club system, no matter for what purpose. The makings of it may be found among the Freideutsche Jugend," the very group before which he was to deliver "Politics as a Vocation" within a few days.[25]

"Politics as a Vocation," then, was delivered at the very moment when Weber's long-standing advocacy of Germany's "responsibility before history" lost its political foundation and the Allied assertion of the German responsibility for the war became the justification of the impending Versailles treaty. If in his Munich address Weber took the high road of a formal defense of the ethic of responsibility, a few weeks later (in March 1919), in the heat of battle that does not permit any distinction between "principled" and "responsible" action, he called, before students and faculty at the University of Heidelberg, for a national uprising against the proposed Versailles treaty. But again a few weeks later, he agreed with great reluctance to accompany the German delegation to Versailles, where he co-authored the German "white book" that rejected the thesis of German responsibility for the war. He puzzled over the many pros and cons, but was finally unable to make up his mind as to whether the treaty should be officially approved. Neither "unprincipled" nor "responsible" reasoning helped him clarify his own attitude toward this crucial decision, which sealed the fate of the nascent Weimar Republic. Shortly before the signing of the treaty on June 28, Weber admitted: "I confess that I am at a complete loss politically. Personally I would favor rejection, no matter what the danger. But I suppose that there will then be a plebiscite that will accept the peace, and this I regard as the worst thing, because it would tie us down so much morally. The whole matter can make one absolutely sick with rage and despair."²⁶ Soon Weber was to fall politically silent and to return to his scholarly studies for the few months left in his life.

4. Constants and Changes in the European Balance of Power

It we read Weber's political writings with our own problems in mind, we can notice several important constants and changes.

1. Most obviously, states and their alliances have remained the dominant actors on the world stage. In this regard Weber's notion of responsible political action, which proceeds from the fact and the interests of the nation state, remains applicable. The democratic mode of government, which for Weber provides the best institutional matrix for responsible action, was imposed on the western part of Germany. With outside aid West German history was forced in a direction which Weber had hoped would be an independent achievement. The Federal Republic has been able to identify with the liberal and democratic traditions of the Rhineland.

2. Weber's theory of imperialism has a notable weakness. His prediction that a lost war would be followed by a long period of German economic decline was upheld only conditionally after the First World War and not at all after the second. During the Korean War, which strained the capacity of the American economy, Japan and West Germany could enter the world market under their American umbrella and embark on a triumphant economic expansion. West Germany seemed to be developing into a pacified and well-administered country that was preoccupied with reconstruction -- in line with Weber's view that a country need not be a Machtstaat if it only wants to be governed well. At any rate, West Germany no longer needed to pursue a world policy in Weber's sense in order to promote its economic interests -- the United States conducted such a policy for its allies, including the losers of the Second World War.

3. Nevertheless, the Federal Republic, unlike Japan, has become a Machtstaat again, if against the wishes of some of its founders. Economic strength and available manpower were, however, less important than the fact that geographic location imposed on the Federal Republic a key role in NATO defense strategy. Still, sheer size played some role. Although seventy, now sixty (and soon fewer) million Germans are no longer perceived as a fatefully large population in Weber's sense, the Federal government self-consciously carries again a larger "responsibility before history" than the smaller NATO partners, whether Norway and Denmark or the Netherlands and Belgium,

which in 1982 were either undecided about the NATO double resolution or wanted to reduce their military burdens. In the wake of the Second World War the notion of German historical responsibility turned into an acknowledgment of German responsibility for mass murder and genocide. Weber had rejected the Allied thesis of German war guilt for the first war, but after the second no evasion was possible. Chancellor Schmidt has repeatedly pointed to the Federal Republic's obligation to reassure the Soviet Union that it will never be threatened again. At the same time the peace movement has drawn on the German responsibility for war crimes and holocaust as a moral argument for a special German obligation to help avoid the conflagrations of modern war everywhere.

4. Weber's hope that the United States would not have to share world domination with Russia has not been fulfilled, as he himself feared. Tocqueville's famous prediction that the world would be divided between the two powers has been correct, although it did not assume the military partitioning of Europe and foresee the impact of military technology on the division of the world. Tocqueville once called the emergence of a vast United States, in which one day one hundred and fifty million people would live, "a fact new to the world, a fact that the imagination strives in vain to grasp."[27] Today our imagination strives in vain to grasp the prospect that one hundred and fifty million or more people in the United States or Europe might perish in a nuclear war.

5. The division of Germany has restored a situation in which "one side would be a Rheinbundstaat (Rhenish Federation State) and the other a Russian satrapy, which would be allowed to fight for, or to be the battleground for, French [read today: western] and Russian interests."[28] But in view of the destructiveness of the nuclear weapons the time seems to have passed for Europe when war can be considered the continuation of politics with other means and "the inevitability of a violent power struggle" must be taken into account.[29] Today when the NATO countries are frustrated about the difficulties of positively influencing the course of events in Poland and elsewhere in eastern Europe, Tocqueville's responsible politics may appear more adequate to us than Weber's, apart from their shared readiness to conduct war.

> After deep reflection ... I adopted two maxims of conduct, which were of great use to me during my brief term as minister of Foreign Affairs, and which, I think, should be followed by anybody in charge of France's external relations in the age in which we live. The first was unreservedly to break with the revolutionary party abroad ... A second maxim was never to attempt anything

obviously beyond our powers; never to promise
what we could not perform; not to encourage
those we could not support, or threaten those we
could not strike... 'Gentlemen,' I said to the
ambassadors on the first occasion when they came
to see me, 'I am no diplomat, and I will say my
last word at the very start and after that change
nothing. I know that France is in no state to
dominate Europe and make her wishes prevail in
distant lands. Therefore we shall not attempt
that. You can count on us leaving you perfectly
free in matters beyond our scope, for we shall
not worry about making ourselves look important... But in bordering countries and on question that affect her directly, France has the right
to exercise not just great but preponderant
influence. We will not meddle in what happens at
the far end of Europe, in the Principalities, in
Poland, or in Hungary. But I warn you that you
cannot do anything in Belgium, Switzerland, or
Piedmont without our advice and concurrence.
There we shall not limit ourselves to negotiation
but will, if need be, go to war, risking everything to keep our position. I am not trying to
hide the fact that a foreign war would be very
difficult and dangerous for us at this moment, for
the whole social structure might break under the
strain, sweeping away our fortunes and our lives.
Nevertheless, you must realize that, in the case I
mentioned, we would even go to war.[30]

6.   There are today two basic strategies from which their
proponents expect a lessening of the dangers of war. One is
NATO's defense strategy. Here we can draw on Weber's balance
of power approach -- remember the Wilson episode above -- and
put it on the scales in favor of "responsible" politics. The
counter-strategy is the renunciatin of the status of a Machtstaat
and some form of neutralization. This appeared as "Swissification" to Weber and is today called "Finlandization." Weber
spoke of "the will to powerlessness in domestic politics preached
by the literati," a rhetoric which contrasted with their noisily
proclaimed "will to power" in the world.[31] Today we encounter
a broader movement toward relative "powerlessness in foreign
affairs." To the Weberian Raymond Aron the pacifist reactions
to some of President Reagan's public statements appear as "out-
bursts of feeling which, in the last analysis, express an almost
unconscious wish -- we do not want to be defended: we accept
the risk of falling under Soviet domination, rather than the risk,
small though it may be, of a war which might turn nuclear. We
met this state of mind thirty years ago in the early 1950s, when

the Korean War was raging: it expressed itself then (as now) in the slogan 'Better red than dead.'"[32] Many people, however, hold positions somewhere in between the NATO double resolution of 1979 and the plea for unilateral disarmament. Let us see whether clear dividing lines between "responsibility" and "good intentions" can be identified.

5. Weber's Two Ethics Today: "Our Responsibility for History"

The polarization of the West German public between the Federal government and a majority of popular opinion as measured by surveys, on the one hand, and the growing opposition movement on the other has found expression also in the utilization of Weberian categories.[33] Chancellor Schmidt himself has relied on Weber's ethic of responsibility in his replies to Christian pacifist critics. For instance, in 1981 he responded in the following way to the question of which ethical principles guided him instead of the Sermon on the Mount: "I have often cited Weber's distinction between the ethics of conviction and the ethic of responsibility. Whoever must decide for others must take responsibility, at least in a democracy. He must make a decision before God or, if it sounds more modest, before his own conscience.... He must take responsibility for the consequences affecting everybody, not merely for the sincerity of his personal motives. Those who advocate the laying down of arms err by equating the sincerity of their motives with the success of their policies.... They adhere to a naive ethic of conviction, which foregoes reason and experience, and are content with the feeling that they face the future with good intentions and leave to God, the lord of history, the consequences resulting from their actions, for which they don't want to be responsible."[34]

The Reverend Heinrich Albertz, formerly lord mayor of Berlin, answered Schmidt in "Die Zeit:" "In the dispute about whether one can govern on the basis of the Sermon on the Mount you refer once again to Weber's distinction between the ethic of conviction and the ethic of responsibility. I too could not govern directly with this sermon when I held an office that involves much less responsibility than yours. Nevertheless, I struggled not to let the sermon deteriorate into a rule for crazies and dreamers. I consider Weber's distinction wrong and dangerous. With it one can ultimately justify every political decision. I fear that those lose increasingly their grip on reality who support the production, stationing and use of atomic weapons as a means of defense and of saving the peace.... More and more I have the impression that the basic rules of the life and teaching of Jesus are our only chance for survival, also as a nation."[35]

In the "principled" view of Christian pacifism, the Federal Republic and its political leadership must stand morally condemned, just as for Chancellor Schmidt the Christian ethic fails to be "responsible." In my view, even today Weber's paired concept can serve us fairly well to bring out the differences between elected political leaders and Christian pacifists as well as anarchists and terrorists. The former attempt to assess the consequences of their actions in the context of the political and military balance of power, the latter act out of sheer conviction and single-minded commitment. Chancellor Schmidt uses Weber's distinction consistently and to good advantage, but its very neatness tends to obscure the fact that there are very few Christian pacifists or terrorists, for that matter. A very large number of citizens, whether they count themselves as members of the peace movement or not, share the Reverend Albertz's fears about the nuclear arms race, without thinking of the Sermon on the Mount. Christian pacifism, which continues the anti-institutional tradition of German pietism, is only one force that works against the Federal government's "responsible" policies. Increasingly important are the fear of a military showdown and the burden of military defense, which is felt more and more as the economic crisis deepens. West Germany's special vulnerability in case of any kind of military conflict is bound to produce "secular" anxieties in their own right. This makes it possible for men like Albertz to speak of the Federal Republic as a Rheinbundstaat almost in Weber's sense.[36] The phrase conjures up the image of a politically and militarily dependent country, which is mired in philistinism and materialism. Recently a tiny number of intellectuals have begun dreaming of a united socialist Germany, which would be neutral between the two great powers. Politically more potent is the increasing feeling of many young people that they live in an occupied country and therefore cannot determine their own future. The government's insistence that the Allied NATO troops are stationed by treaty appears to some young people as a legalistic argument. The derogatory phrase "this republic" has taken on a connotation similar to the expression "the system," with which the Weimar Republic was once denounced. To the degree that the Nazi period and the Second World War recede in memory -- and they are a personal experience only for those over fifty -- judgments about the Federal Republic are no longer based on comparisons with a horrible past. Unhistorical yardsticks tend to displace comparative historical experience. Stalinism, too, is remembered less and less. Moreover, since the years of Stalinist totalitarianism life under Communism has indeed lost some of its terrors and thus makes "better red than dead" sound less like a council of despair. Many people in eastern Europe seem able to have a private life of sorts. Indeed, a strict separation of the realm of state and private life seems to have become a characteristic of Communist systems. The Polish Catholic church has stood up to Communist secularism, and even in the GDR a small Pietist movement has come into being. Hungarian "goulash socialism" seems to have made political conditions bearable for a large part of the population. Insofar as the economic conditions do not improve or even deteriorate, this can be attributed not only to socialist inefficiency but also the general crisis of the capitalist world system.

What has changed decisively since Weber spoke of "our responsibility before history" is not the division of the world between America and Russia or the demise of the German nation state after only seventy-five years, but the sudden dawn of the nuclear age. Now the survival of populations, not of nation states is at stake -- a situation not anticipated by Weber. It is quite possible that many millions, perhaps hundreds of millions, will die because of rational strategic decisions by political and military leaders. Thus, to Weber's view of the harsh realities of international power politics must be added the new reality of a danger to the survival of whole populations.

Before the First World War pacifism in Germany was propagated by a handful of writers. Afterwards the "Nie wieder Krieg" ("Never again war") movement was supported by masses of people who had experienced the horrors of the "Great War." Today pacifism is no longer a matter of "a few pacifist utopians" or of a generation which suffered through a world war. With the prospect of nuclear annihilation pacifism in a broad sense has attained an entirely new historical significance. The very term "peace movement" denotes a movement larger than the pacifism of the past. If the new kind of pacifism is no longer just a humanitarian movement aiming at a "world without war," but is struggling to assure the very survival of the human race, then it is equally a matter of good intentions and of responsibility. Finally, the question might even been raised whether in the extreme "better red than dead" could appear as the ultimate ethic of responsibility, whereas "better dead than red" could look like a stubborn ethic of conviction. Whereas surrender under the threat of nuclear devastation might very well make sense to West European leaders, if it should ever come to that point, no elected leader can be expected to face the alternative in advance. Chancellor Schmidt has prudently tried to avoid being pinned down to this alternative: "We have a concrete conscience and not a theoretical conscience. Moral issues are decided at the time and in the circumstances when they come up for a decision.... It is the responsibility of German security and foreign policy, that is, of German peace policy, to avoid a situation in which one's own people and one's own state are forced into an alternative between two decisions: whether to submit to slavery or to die. And if you wish to force me into assuming that this policy could fail completely, then I must say that one cannot answer such hypothetical questions with complete validity for everyone. I may add that I consider such hypothetical situations improbable and, indeed, I am convinced that we shall succeed in avoiding such alternatives."[37]

37

This is an exemplary answer for an elected leader, who has the constitutional responsibility to protect the basic liberties of the people. The context of the statement, however, was the controversy about the NATO defense strategy, particularly the double resolution of 1979, which Schmidt has championed as a "responsible" policy. Critics point to a range of diplomatic and military alternatives which appear to them as "responsible" as the present NATO policy, if not less risky for ultimate survival. Below the level of an ultimate choice between being red or dead, there are, after all, a number of serious arguments that can be considered by both sides. The strategic reasoning behind the balance of terror can be challenged on instrumental rather than principled grounds. The United States has always relied on a policy of staying one step ahead of the Soviet Union in a technological race that cannot be won in the long run. NATO strategy has been morally compromised by its willingness to use nuclear weapons first, if deemed necessary to hold off conventional Soviet forces. The NATO double resolution was meant to be an effective ploy for striking a deal with the Soviet Union, but it has become a source of much tension within the alliance and the cause of severe domestic strains in several countries. The trouble is that every new round in the armament race introduces more "sophisticated" weapons that are more deadly, more accurate and harder to detect, cutting the time for counter-measures to seconds rather than minutes. Mutual destruction is assured ever more certainly, if human misjudgment occurs. As a sense of puzzlement and perplexity is spreading among leaders and led, the peace movement is propelled by the perception that the long-range success of the NATO leaders' "responsible" policies is more and more uncertain. But the European peace movement also knows that it cannot bring about nuclear disarmament on a global scale. It can perhaps defeat the NATO double resolution and even undermine NATO altogether, but it cannot prevent the continued nuclear confrontation between the two superpowers. Forcing the United States back into an isolationist stance could even increase the dangers of war. Thus, the pacifists too must weigh the consequences of their actions, unless they are willing to weaken or defeat their own cause.

Weber could take it for granted that there would be generational succession and hence history in the future. We cannot do so any more. This creates a special kind of responsibility not before our descendants, but for the very possibility that new generations will be able to live -- a new ethical situation eloquently described by Jonathan Schell in his recent book.[38] It seems to me that the desperate efforts of many elected leaders and peace groups today are not a matter of an ethic of responsibility versus an ethic of conviction but of different responsible attempts to save the future. In contrast to Weber's polar concepts, his battle-cry "our responsibility before history" has not remained part of public memory. Perhaps it should be resurrected today with a changed emphasis as a peaceable call to take responsibility not <u>before</u>, but <u>for</u> history, since after a nuclear holocaust there may be no more future for Europe, the West or the whole world.

NOTES

[1] In the famous passage on "the iron cage" in The Protestant Ethic and the Spirit of Capitalism Weber points out that "the tremendous cosmos of the modern economic order... will determine the lives of all the individuals who are born into this mechanism... perhaps... until the last ton of fossilized fuel has been burnt." See Weber, The Protestant Ethic and the Spirit of Capitalism, T. Parsons tr. (New York: Scribner, 1958), p.181. For Weber's critique of Wilhelm Ostwald's belief that there will be no scarcity of energy sources in the future and his own view that our energy resources could be exhausted "in little more than a thousand years if exploitation increases at its present rate," see his last untranslated "methodological" critique, "'Energetische' Kulturtheorien" (1909), Wissenschaftslehre, Joh. Winckelmann ed. (Tubingen:Mohr, 1951), p. 409.

[2] Max Weber, "Parlament und Regierung im neugeordneten Deutschland" (May 1918), Gesammelte politische Schriften, Joh. Winckelmann ed. (Tubingen:Mohr, 1971), 3rd. enl. ed., p. 443; abbreviated below as PS. The passage is from the last section not included in translation of the essay in the appendix to Weber, Economy and Society, G. Roth and Claus Wittich eds. (Berkeley:University of California Press, 1978), pp. 1318-1469.

[3] See my introduction to Wolfgang Schluchter, The Rise of Western Rationalism: Max Weber's Developmental History (Berekely:University of California Press, 1981), pp. vx-xxvii.

[4] See "Politik als Beruf," PS, pp. 505-560; From Max Weber, H. H. Gerth and C. W. Mills eds. (New York: Oxford University Press, 1946), pp. 77-128.

[5] See Wolfgang Schluchter, "Value-Neutrality and the Ethic of Responsibility," in Roth and Schluchter, Max Weber's Vision of History: Ethics and Methods, (Berkeley: University of California Press, 1971), pp. 65-116.

[6] See Schluchter, The Rise of Western Rationalism, op. cit., pp. 39-66.

[7] "Die Zeit," January 8, 1982, p. 6 and January 29, 1982, p. 1.

[8]"Politics as a Vocation," op. cit., p. 77.

[9]In general, the situational aspect of Weber's analysis has not interested American readers. "Politics as a Vocation" has been assigned to (probably) hundred of thousands of American students as an introduction to the sociology of domination and the ethos of politics, but not as a warning against pacifism and revolutionary romanticism.

[10]"Politics as a Vocation," op. cit., p. 119. On p. 126 Weber quotes from Goethe's Faust: "The devil is old. Grow old to understand him." This phrase is repeated in "Science as a Vocation" (op. cit., p. 152). Both passages are marred by translation errors. Read "the" instead of "two diabolical forces" on p. 126, line 10 from below. The second error has given rise to some serious misinterpretations of Weber. By affirming "science as a vocation," Weber rejects, of course, "the standpoint that hates intellectualism as the worst devil, as youth does today;" he is not speaking "from precisely the standpoint that hates intellectualism" (P. 152, line 16 from below).

[11]Weber, "Zwischen zwei Gesetzen" (Feb. 1916), PS, p. 144f. Cf. my "Weber's generational Rebellion and Maturation," in Reinhard Bendix and G. R., Scholarship and Partisanship (Berkeley: University of California Press, 1971), p. 28. My emphasis.

[12]Weber, "Zur Grundung einer national-sozialen Partei" (Nov. 1896), PS, p. 28f.

[13]"Politics as a Vocation," op. cit., p. 126.

[14]An echo of Weber's political position is found, appropriately enough, in his discussion of the nation in Economy and Society, op. cit., p. 921f.: "The attachment to... political prestige may fuse with a specific belief in responsibility toward succeeding generations. The great power structures per se are then held to have a responsibility of their own for the way in which power and prestige are distributed between their own and foreign polities."

[15]Weber, "Der Nationalstaat und die Volkswirtschaftspolitik" (May 1895), PS, pp. 12, 14, 23f. Weber's emphasis. Weber continued: "Our generation is not fortunate enough to know whether its struggle will bear fruit (as the nation-builders of 1870 knew) and whether posterity will accept us as its ancestors. We shall not succeed in banning the spell cast on us -- to be the epigones of a great political era -- unless we succeed in becoming something else -- precursors

of an even greater one. Will this be our place in history? I don't know, and merely say: It is the right of youth to be true to itself and to its ideals. It is not the passage of years that makes man senile; he remains young as long as he can feel the great passions with which nature has endowed us."

[16]On the ethical culture movement, see now Horace L. Friess, Felix Adler and Ethical Culture: Memories and Studies, Fannia Weingartner ed. (New York: Columbia University Press, 1981); the phrase "zoological nationalism" is cited in Marianne Weber, Max Weber, tr. Harry Zohn (New York: Wiley, 1975), p. 412.

[17]"Zwischen zwei Gesetzen," PS, p. 142.

[18]"Stellungnahme zur Flottenumfrage" (Jan. 1898), PS, p. 30.

[19]See Gerhard Hufnagel, Kritik als Beruf. Der kritische Gehalt im Werk Max Webers (Berling: Ullstein, 1971). See also M. Rainer Lepsius, "Kritik als Beruf. Zur Soziologie der Intellektuellen," Kolner Zeitschrift fur Soziologie, 16:1 (1964): 75-91.

[20]"Zwischen zwei Gesetzen," PS, p. 143. My emphasis.

[21]"Deutschland unter den europaischen Weltmachten" (Oct. 1916), PS, p. 176f. My emphasis.

[22]"Wahlrecht und Demokratie in Deutschland" (Dec. 1917), PS, p. 282f.; From Max Weber, op. cit., p. 390f.

[23]"Waffenstillstand und Frieden" (Oct. 27, 1918), PS, p. 447.

[24]Quoted in Marianne Weber, op. cit., p. 636f.

[25]Loc. cit.

[26]Op. cit., p. 657.

[27]Alexis de Tocqueville, Democracy in America, Phillips Bradley ed. (New York: Vintage, 1960), I, p. 452.

[28]"Deutschland unter den europaischen Weltmachten," PS, p. 177.

[29]"Zwischen zwei Gesetzen," PS, p. 145.

[30]Alexis de Tocqueville, Recollections, J. P. Mayer and A. P. Kerr eds. (Garden City: Doubleday, 1971), p. 298f.

[31]"Parlament und Reierung," PS, p. 442.

[32]Raymond Aron, "Diplomatic Double-Think," Encounter, Jan. 1982, p. 38f.

[33]For opinion poll results on the "fierce struggle for public opinion... going on in West Germany at the moment... in fact, a kind of theatre of war," see Elisabeth Noelle-Neumann, "Are the Germans 'Collapsing' or 'Standing Firm'?" Encounter, Feb. 1982, p. 76ff. (On the "swift recovery of belief in the Soviet Union's good intentions" in spite of the invasion of Afghanistan, see p. 78.) On the composition of the peace movement and the tendencies of youthful protest, see Gunther Schmid, "Zur Soziologie der Friedensbewegung und des Jugendprotests," Aus Politik und Zeitges chichte, supplement to "Das Parlament," June 19, 1982, pp. 15-30. See also Wilfred von Bredow, "Zusammensetzung und Ziele der Friedensbewegung in der Bundesrepublik Deutschland," op. cit., pp. 3-13.

[34]Interview with Chancellor Helmut Schmidt in Evangelische Kommentare, 14:4 (April 1981): 214 and 216. Schmidt took the same line in a debate with young people at the bi-annual Protestant Church Congress in Hamburg on June 19, 1981, before a nationwide television audience - an event hardly conceivable in the United States:
"Question: May I ask you a very personal question? How do you in your capacity as Federal Chancellor view political responsibility? You passionately endorse Nato's double resolution ...?"
Schmidt: "Nobody can be sure that he is doing the right thing.... The result of a non-decision can also be wrong. Those who imagine that they can foretell the future course of events are moving far away from the Christian view of life. God is the Master of History, as they say.... This does not relieve us of our responsibility - neither you nor me. But you seem to believe that it is irresponsible to adopt such resolutions. (Interjection by a panelist: "It is at the present time.") That is your opinion, and I would like to say a few words about it. There was a reference to the Sermon on the Mount. This Sermon affirms, for example, that one should not resist those who do us harm. ...One cannot simply take the easy way out by saying that one will accept a situation whereby the others build up their armaments and target their rockets on my city and on other cities, and I shall simply rely on my hope that God will provide for me. That is not possible. We must also bear some of the responsibility. At the same time, we here in the West must show the other side that we are prepared to defend ourselves if anyone tries to harm us. This is the

basis of the non-war of the last three and a half decades since 1945. It rests on the fact - and this is very difficult to grasp - that each side is capable of [destroying the other].... That is the equilibrium of terror.... Those who cannot defend themselves will suffer the same fate as the Afghans."
From Statement and Speeches. New York: German Information Center, IV:12, July 7, 1981, p. 4.

[35]Quoted from the reprint in Henirich Albertz, Blumen fur Stukenbrock (Stuttgart: Radiusverlag, 1981), p. 224. See also the similar comments on Schmidt and Weber in an interview with Evangelische Kommentare, 14:8 (Aug. 1981): 457-460. Walter Jens, one of the leading leftwing intellectuals, president of the German PEN club and professor of rhetoric at the University of Tubingen, extolled Albertz at the expense of Schmidt, whom he accused of having talked at the Protestant Church Congress in 1981 like a public accountant presenting a balance sheet at a meeting of corporate stockholders. Jens claimed that the perspective of men like Albertz is less Christian than Jesus-centered. He applauded Albertz's insistence that the Sermon on the Mount is a political fact and quoted a sentence omitted by Albertz in the reprint of his article: "If the rulers do not have enough imagination to visualize what a future war would mean, then a Christian must point to the misery of the Third World in order to demonstrate what the arms race mentality is perpetuating right now: the Bethlehemite murder of the children of a large part of the world -- and tomorrow it could happen everywhere." Walter Jens, "Ein Prediger in der Wuste," Der Spiegel, Jan. 26, 1982, p. 159.

[36]Albertz, op. cit., p. 15.

[37] Statements and Speeches, New York: German Information Center, IV:12, July 7, 1981, p. 10f.

[38]See Jonathan Schell, The Fate of the Earth (New York: Knopf, 1981).

Discussion

BIERSTEDT: Let me say, first of all, that it is a pleasure to be participating with such noted authorities on Max Weber as Guenther Roth and David Little. I only wish that such Weberian scholars from the past, friends of mine like the later Alexander von Schelting, author of Max Weber's Wissenschaftslehre, and Johannes Winckelmann, keeper of the Weber archives in Munich and a wonderful gentleman who spoke English with an Indiana twang, could also be with us. And of course another friend, Reinhard Bendix, also belongs to this estimable company.

Let me say secondly - and here I suppose I will startle you - that I am slightly iconoclastic about Weber, who is now perhaps at the apogee of his fame. I am not sure that the corpus of his work altogether merits the high praise it has received. In the first place, Weber did not produce a system of sociology, a task that I regard as a necessary one for a socio- logical theorist to undertake. In the second place, he was one of the most disorganized of sociologists, an opinion supported even by his wife, Marianne. Of course, he became a sociologist posthumously, so to speak (in the United States at least), not with the English translation of his General Economic History by Frank Knight in 1927, the first English translation of his work, but with the translation and publication, in 1930, by Talcott Parsons, of The Protestant Ethic and the Spirit of Capitalism. I have much admiration for The Protestant Ethic. It seems to me, in spite of the healthy controversy that has surrounded it, and in spite of its long list of critics, that it is a major contribution to the ideological interpretation of history and of social change. No one knows, incidentally, whether its thesis is true. We judge it not by its "truth," but rather by its cogency, and here I give high marks indeed to the sage of Heidelberg. On bur- eaucracy, however, Weber may not be telling us anything that we did not already know.

I reserve comment on the many other subjects to which Weber directed his attention - with two exceptions. In a re- cently published book I have endeavored to show that all of the most prominent American sociologists, from Sumner through Merton, subscribed to the notion of a value-free sociology. None of them needed the German word Wertfreiheit to argue their case and none of them relied on Weber's famous essay, "Science as a Vocation," to support it. Indeed, until we come, in chrono- logical order, to Parsons, we find few references to Weber by those whose statues occupy a place in the American Pantheon.

Finally, although this observation depends upon the diffi- culty of translating the German word Herrschaft, Weber's ty- pology of three forms of authority - traditional, rational-legal, and charismatic - is almost certainly erroneous. Traditional authority and rational-legal authority are clearly forms of authority, but charismatic authority is not authority at all, but rather a form of leadership - and on this, perhaps insignificant, point, I am happy to say that Reinhard Bendix agrees with me. There is a cluster of concepts - influence, dominance, competence, force, power, authority, and leadership - that tend to get tangled up in an unmanageable knot of semantic confusion.

It is time, however, to respond to Guenther Roth's superior paper. He begins by suggesting that not Marx, not Durkheim, not Weber, could have anticipated the horror of a world in which Einstein's famous equation -- - $E = Mc^2$ -- would be translated into practical reality. For some reason, like lemmings rushing to extinction, we seem to prefer nuclear incineration to the surrender of national sovereignty. Durkheim, alone of the three, spoke favorably of a world community and a world government, but he did so almost incidentally, and without any hope that such an ideal could be realized. Indeed, in this situation, one that could consume us all, and unborn generations as well, Saint-Simon was more sanguine than Durkheim. I agree with Roth's judgment that Weber did not envisage such a world as we are forced to tolerate today. He could not have done so, and in any case he was a German patriot. I agree with Roth also -- although in a way that is tragic to contemplate -- that Weber's distinction between the ethic of responsibility and the ethic of conviction, in "Politics as a Vocation," is a rudimentary sketch, not a systematic analysis." One nuclear missile, finding its target, would destroy the distinction. Finally, I agree with both Weber and Roth that there is a tension between value-freedom in science and moral responsibility in politics. I remember the remarkable perspicacity of Saint-Simon who, early in the nineteenth century, wrote of the scientists, "All Europe is in a death-struggle: what are you doing to stop this butchery? Nothing. It is you who perfect the means of destruction." There are some among us, myself not included, who advocate a moratorium on science. Unfortunately, what has now been done cannot be undone. The causal chain does not run backwards.

Unfortunately, my insufficient knowledge of German history does not permit me to comment on the situation that Weber confronted in 1919. We are all "tied to the realities of this world," as Weber so eloquently said, and we are all unable to think, as Weber also said, beyond the reality of our own graves. We too have a "damned duty before history." We too have our responsibilities and, whether theist or non-theist, must take communion before the altar of history.

STRONG: I think I come to a conference on leadership with a considerable handicap having recently been trained as a political scientist. As a group political scientists have particular problems in dealing with the concept of leadership. The explanation for that is quite obvious. The central concept for political science is power and the central question asked about power is, who has it. When Aristotle, who used to hold interdisciplinary conferences like this one by talking to himself, sat down and made the first classification of political regimes, he did so on the basis of two criteria. His first question was who rules, and his answer was the one, the few, or the many. His second question was do the rulers act in their own interest or the common interest, and that gave him his famous catalog of six regimes: tyranny and kingship, oligarchy and aristocracy, democracy and polity. Democracy was of course the bad form of popular rule. Political scientists have not gone very far since Aristotle, and as a matter of fact we have probably regressed. We no longer pay much attention to whether or not rulers act in accordance with the common interest, and spend most of our time trying to discover the locus of power in the particular nations, institutions and organizations which we study. We even assume that we find out who has power by first finding out what the distribution of wealth, status, and other values is in a given group or society. This is the clear implication of Lasswell's famous definition of politics as the study of "who gets what, when and how." Though a few political scientist have studied leadership, most recently James MacGregor Burns, most have ignored it, or cynically treated it as a form of manipulation applied by rulers upon the ruled.

Max Weber offers two important corrections to this defect in political science. First, he turns the whole question of "Who rules?" completely on its head, and asks instead, "Why does anyone ever obey?" Answering this question gives us his famous classifications of types of authority -- traditional, charismatic, and legal-rational. Weber's second contribution to the study of leadership is the distinction analyzed in Professor Roth's paper between the ethic of conviction and the ethic of responsibility. This is an important subject since it restores concern for the relationship between political leadership and the moral character of political action, a concern which has been missing, at least among political scientists, for some time.

Professor Roth suggests that the existence of nuclear weapons may have changed European pacificism, which Weber earlier in this century would have classified as an ethic of conviction, into an ethic of responsibility. This is a provocative thesis, and while I cannot refute it, I do have two reservations: the first concerns the character of European nuclear protest, the second deals with the moral dilemmas inherent in the nuclear age.

I am not convinced that the European nuclear protest movement is a pacificist movement. I am more familiar with the nuclear protest organizations in Britain than I am with those in Germany, and, at least in the British example, it is clear that many participants in nuclear protest organizations do not have a particular philosophy or program, pacificist or otherwise. Frank

Parkins, a British sociologist who studied the British nuclear protestors following Bertrand Russel in the 1950s concludes that they were individuals interested in "expressive politics" rather than "instrumental politics." They wanted to vent their frustration, their rage, their disgust with the political situation faced by the world in a nuclear age. They were never really serious about taking any political action in response to that situation. A group of sociologists have done similar research on the current protest movement in Britain and come to more or less the same conclusion. You can find additional evidence for this idea in at least some of the comments made by Russell and E. P. Thompson, the leaders of the former and current British disarmament campaigns. There were times when they were pressed by reporters, when they took their arguments to logical conclusions, when they admitted that in fact the disarmament movement they were engaged in was probably futile. Even if Britain unilaterally disarmed, even if Europe became neutral, the United States and the Soviet Union would still possess nuclear weapons, there would still be disputes in the Middle East, Africa and elsewhere. No matter what is done nuclear war is likely to occur. Russell says this in a number of his books and points out that there are two consequences for such a war; everyone in the northern hemisphere will die, and the world will then be run by Australians and South Africans, a clear triumph for the "free world." E. P. Thompson is also something of a fatalist on this subject and is almost compelled to be because his arguments describe a desperate situation. We are on the brink of nuclear war, accidents are likely to happen at any moment, irrational leaders can and do come to power. These statements so exaggerate the perils of the nuclear age that it is almost impossible for nuclear protesters to believe that their movement will do any good. Thompson says, in one article, that if nuclear war occurred it probably would not be good for the South Africans but it might at least save the whales. So that is one reservation about Professor Roth's paper. The European protest movement against nuclear weapons may be neither evidence of an ethic of conviction or an ethic of responsibility, and it may instead be an expression of resignation. That's not a reservation that I particularly care for. It makes the protests in some sense trivial and irrelevant to the development of policy. But on the other hand I see problems with Professor Roth's suggestion that the solution is pacificism.

My second reservation is really Henry Kissinger's position on these issues, which might be classified as an attempt to exercise Weber's ethic of responsibility for the nuclear issue. Let me just read one Kissinger quote and then stop. "When nations are able to inflict tens of millions of casualties in a matter of hours, peace has become a moral imperative. But the root dilemma of our time is that if the quest for peace turns into the sole objective of policy, the fear of war becomes a weapon in

the hands of the most ruthless; it produces moral disarmament."
Kissinger's warning is that we cannot unilaterally disarm, we
cannot adopt pacificism as our political strategy. We need to
both resist the Soviet Union and at the same time seriously
engage in arms control. Those are policies which quite properly
are viewed by the European protesters as failed alternatives, but
I think for Kissinger and some other political leaders they would
be offered as responsible policies and really the only alternatives
available in the current situation.
ROTH: Now a word on Strong's last point. If you permit me I
will make an autobiographical remark. I was in many ways an
unreconstructed cold warrior for many years and in favor of
negotiating in a very tough fashion with the Soviet Union. I
have, however, begun to talk more and more with the children
of my political friends in Germany. The paper reflects the
impact of the conversations I had with them, though I have not
made up my mind exactly where I stand in regard to the proposals of the peace movement or Helmut Schmidt's strategy.
Therefore, I do not want to say whether I agree in principle
with Kissinger or not, but what you read to me I accept.
However at the moment, the situation seems to be that the whole
context for discussion has changed. The expectation that SALT
II would be signed by now and there would be an ongoing process of overall disarmament settlement with the Soviet Union has
disappeared. The Reagan administration has pulled back from
negotiations in order to arm first and then negotiate later from a
position of strength. To the extent that the peace movement
puts pressure on the Reagan administration to move toward arms
control without first going through this very questionable massive buildup, to that extent I think the peace movement has an
important function.
FEUER: Roth remarked that he is allergic to Weber's notion of
charisma. And I think Americans generally are allergic to this
notion of charisma. Let us explore the reasons why the concept
does not seem a very fruitful one for analyzing the sources, the
psychology, or the sociology of leadership. Suppose we take a
man who has generally been acknowledged to have a great deal
of charisma. In the twentieth century I suppose Lenin has this
title. Life Magazine during the Second World War devoted a
whole issue to Lenin and said he was undoubtedly the greatest
man of the twentieth century. Now if we look at Lenin's character and personality, we want to know how we can test whether
Lenin had charisma. Suppose we had asked the people who
knew him before 1917 what their opinion was of him. Did they
think he was an unusual personality? Or what did people who
met him immediately after the revolution think of his personal
character? We do have some relevant information in regard to
these questions. The American delegate to the Socialist International, was a man named Robert Hunter, who later wrote a
book reporting his impressions of Lenin, whom he encountered

there.   Hunter states that Lenin attracted almost no attention. There was some feeling that he was probably a Czarist police agent because wherever he went he caused quarrels among people, and was obviously trying to disorganize the party. Other had the same reaction.   Vanderbilt, the Belgian sociologist, who usually chaired the meeting of the International, met Lenin repeatedly, and said he was an utterly colorless person, who made no contribution to the meetings.   Bertrand Russell wrote in a very famous article at the time of the revolution that Lenin was a typical Russian nobleman, cold, calculating, with a contempt for the masses whom he was prepared to use for his own purposes and power in a cruel way.   He conveyed no impression of greatness.   Russell confessed that his blood ran cold when they were talking of the massacres and executions and he said Lenin laughed aloud at the reference to them.

What does all this add up to?   It adds up to the fact that if, as a social scientist, you had tried to administer tests to Lenin as to how much charisma he had, you would have ended up with a rather negative number.   He did not have the charisma that people attributed to him later.   His own followers around the year 1911 had dwindled down to about ten.   He did not have the charisma of a person with a political movement.

We should, therefore, shift our attention.   We should not search for the charisma in a person, as Weber tried to do.   We should rather ask, as Roth indicated, under what historical conditions are people charisma prone.   What are the weaknesses in the psychology of people that make them inclined to read into a character all kinds of divine attributes, when those attributes are not there at all, but simply indicate that the people are longing for some kind of redeemer, some kind of messiah.

People who are charisma-prone, under a great nervous and psychological strain, tend to be drawn to ascetic personalities. Generally speaking, a very large percentage of these charismatic personalities are ascetics.   Gandhi made a great deal of the fact that he was a celebate.   In fact, he and his wife both announced publicly that they would live as brother and sister henceforth, and at once his holiness quotient arose, and people were inclined to find much more charisma in him.   Lenin was above all an ascetic personality, living extremely simply, living at times under extreme poverty.   Even the case of Franklin Delano Roosevelt, during a period when the American people were in a kind of psychological shock, illustrates the point.   The fact that he was disabled by his infantile paralysis had something to do with charisma, his holiness, and caused people to identify him as a redeeming personality more than they would otherwise have done.   While Lincoln was alive, and certainly when he was running for office, people did not find what we call charisma in him. But Lincoln was brought to charismatic dimensions by his martyrdom.   Martyrdom raises a person beyond discussion and endows him with something special.

Now suppose we take a man like Churchill. Churchill emerged as the charismatic personality of the war, but if one goes back, let us say to the year 1932, he would have been regarded, as a person who, although personally popular, didn't have stable ideas, moved from one party to another, was brilliant but unreliable, and who was essentially a journalist, a maker of phrases. But the British people were looking for a leader, and Churchill expressed their hope and determination to resist; consequently he became endowed with charisma.

Charisma is also often ascribed to individuals with a power of life and death over people. And when a person has this power of life and death, as Hitler or Stalin had, this tends to bring out certain reflexes of submission, like a mouse who is being played with by a cat. There is a tendency on the part of all of us to become submissive psychologically in the presence of this awesome power and this is a constituent of the notion of charisma. It is again not present in the person objectively in any sense, but is an accident of a whole social situation or historic situation in which one person achieves such power.

Now all of this brings us to the specific points about Max Weber and the failures of leadership in our time. Here of course Weber unfortunately participated in the greatest failure of leadership in Germany -- of the intellectuals, at any rate. This was in the year 1914. Everybody in Europe expected that the German Social Democratic Party would oppose Germany's going to war. As late as July 30, the German Social Democratic parliamentary group was practically unanimously agreed that they were going to vote against the war credits. They sent a delegate to Paris to consult with the French comrades and to arrive at a common policy. All agreed -- the French Socialists as well as the Germans -- that they would oppose the war. Meanwhile, the Kaiser's government went ahead and declared war, and suddenly the whole situation was transformed psychologically. From virtual unanimity against the war credits, the Social Democrats were now almost unanimously in favor of voting for them. The argument was the same argument Weber used. Europe was being attacked by Russian savages and Marx and Engels always said that the greatest threat to Europe is Russian tyranny, Russian barbarianism, and so on, and there is need to stand up to that. Now there is validity in that argument. But what followed from it was that Germany should have fought the Russians, but not have declared war on France. However, in that atmosphere the Social Democrats went along with the Kaiser's government and made no distinction whatsoever between France and Russia, they accepted the declaration of war on France and they voted for the war credits.

Weber never admitted the inconsistencies of all this. Instead he hid behind phrases like 'responsibility before history.' Whenever a person starts talking of historical missions and 'responsibility before history,' something is getting covered up.

Where he failed was that he simply accepted conventional values. He said German honor must supersede English social conventions, the French sense of reason, and the Russian bureaucratic mentality. But what does this mean? This was the cliche of his society, this was not the responsible action of a sociologist. In addition, Weber never faced the question of German guilt of which he was one of the component parts. Others did. Einstein was prepared to say right from the very beginning in 1914, when he refused to sign the manifesto of the intellectuals, that Germany was guilty, and he even attacked the intellectual leader of the German social democracy for not recognizing German guilt, especially towards France. Weber did not recognize this guilt. He simply accepted, for all his sociological learning, the familiar nationalist categories of his time.

ROTH: I do agree that the category of charisma is much too heterogeneous. But it is helpful to understand that for Weber charisma was not primarily a psychological category of inherent qualities of leadership, but part of an institutional theory of leadership. And there were or course only two kinds in history. There were traditional ways of leading and there was a modern way of leading. We might remove interminable difficulties regarding the use of the term charisma if we simply replace it by the term 'self-legitimization.' Charisma was necessary as a typological component for Weber's sociology of domination. He needed a term, for better or worse, and it may have been for worse, to indicate usurpation, or the revolutionary seizure of power, which then goes through processes of routinization, institutionalization, reversals of one kind or another.

So my emphasis in looking at leaders would not be Feuer's emphasis, namely what people felt when they were in the presence of Lenin, who by the time of the Socialist International, was losing his mind anyhow, and had to be cued in with words he couldn't remember, as eventually happened to Churchill, when he couldn't recall the countries of the empire. Rather what interests me about Churchill, during the war, is the way in which he used emergency powers to conduct a successful, personal rulership. So I am not concerned with any inherent charismatic qualities of Churchill. But in a wartime situation when no elections were possible, when parliament had no proper powers of oversight, he conducted the war with a system of personal rulership. That I do find of sociological interest.

BAILEY: I wish to address the relation of leadership to a capacity for oratory and rhetoric. What is rhetoric and oratory is not necessarily clear thinking at all. On the contrary, such devices typically obscure things by making issues much simpler than they really are. There is within leadership some extra quality and my conviction is that it is a quality which has nothing at all to do with intellectual ability, and that is why academics are not great leaders. They are used to doubting, to asking questions. But leaders have a way of stopping questions, of stopping doubt, and of impelling people to act without thinking.

LITTLE: We need to focus on this problem of the responsibility of leadership that Bailey has been raising and that certainly has been raised by the general discussion of Weber. Bailey's suggestion seems to be that responsibility amounts to effectiveness. In other words, if a leader succeeds in pulling the wool over the people who follow him that amounts to responsibility. Would that be fair?

BAILEY: No, pulling the wool would not be fair. Helping them make up their minds would be a little more fair.

LITTLE: It seemed to me one problem, at least as posed for us by Weber and Roth is the question of what counts as responsibility. We do seem to judge leaders as to whether they are responsible or not, but so far we have not done a very effective job of defining what might count as the standards of responsibility according to which we assess leaders, one way or the other. Weber struggled with that problem, but as has been pointed out, not altogether successfully.

BAILEY: I do not think you can talk about responsibilty until you first define what the goal is. Once you have done that then you can make the man accountable according to whether or not he reaches the goal. But to apply this test simply reveals one's own particular values and nothing else. Was x a good leader? It depends on the way you want the world to be. And there are a dozen different answers to that one.

COHEN: This lead us back to Roth's point that leadership is always institutionally connected, whether in the case of kings or tribal authorities, or democratic leaders. If there is institutional connection then the ends of leadership are connected with the role of the institution at any particular time. If you are the head of the mafia, you have one set of goals, and if you are the President of a democracy you have a quite different set. The role of the leader depends on the relationship between a single figure and what Bailey calls an entourage, but all parties are members of an institution which produces new leaders. So it seems to me that we are involved with two different considerations. One is the historical fact that at different times there are going to be quite different goals of an institution. The second is that theoretically for every leader there is some institution of which the leader is a part. Whether there is any single goal, that seems to me historically most unlikely.

THOMPSON: Is not there also a distinction in Weber between social theory and the problem of the citizen? In some of his writings he gives the impression that the peculiar problem of the citizen is in acting in a sphere that lies beyond the scholar's tidy systems and frameworks of thought, and that is made up of many contingent factors and imponderables. So he does not argue for value-free action by the citizen in the way that he does for the thinker. And in that sense Weber is different in his approach to say Horkheimer and Adorno who, at a critical moment in history with the Nazis at the gate of domination of Europe argued about fine points in Marxist doctrine. In other words, Weber was aware, as they may not have been, at least in that stage, and as theorists of all brands are not aware, of the intimate need of the citizen to make judgements where broad categories are at best rough indicators and where one has to make approximate choices. I think that is a difference.

The other thing worth noting is that some leaders seem to come into a crisis with a framework and a capacity to cope, while others seem to have only the most trivial framework. Compare for example the general speeches of Ronald Reagan with the early writings of Churchill. There are almost no themes that Churchill discusses in the history of the war that are not present in the early writing -- the relation between the political and the military, the role of the diplomat, the place of force and strength. Everything is there in the early writings. And he then calls these themes into play, wisely or unwisely, vaingloriously or not, when he has responsibility. Kissinger does the same thing, whether one likes him or not. He has some propositions that he uses when he tries to justify detente or justify anything else. There are some genuine substantive issues that are before the group here, represented by the notions of responsibility, accountability and history. Anthropologists refer repeatedly to the notion of context: e.g., Bailey explained that in certain contexts especially the charismatic leader may emerge. But it is more than that. I think we need to hear Roth indicate in what ways the German notion of history is involved. Somebody spoke the phrase concrete history. What is concrete history? Currently a lot is invested in this and related phrases. Phrases like responsibility and accountability are by no means merely phrases interesting to Weberians, but are used as well by economists, political scientists, public administrators and even some anthropologists. So it seems we need to understand more of what is being said.

GUARDIANS AND PRINCES:
STRATEGIES FOR THE CONTROL OF AN ENTOURAGE
F. G. Bailey

Introduction[1]

Effective leaders whose power rests partly upon the services they command from bureaucracies, nevertheless behave in
ways that defy canons of good bureaucratic conduct, such as
orderliness, cooperation and impersonality. Worse than that,
all effective leaders, whether dependent on bureaucracies or not,
often fail to exhibit that peculiar quality which is supposed to
distinguish leadership: virtue. At least that is true if virtue
means "moral excellence:" if the word is given its ancient
meaning -- bravery -- and one passes down the line from
"brave" to "bold" to "ruthless," then effective leaders do have
virtue. Their conduct must transcend ordinary limitations, both
of rationality and of decency. An effective leader must break
rules.

I will give substance to these tendentious assertions by
focusing on one of the tasks of leadership -- how to control
followers. For the present, control over followers will be used
as a measure of an effective leader, and we take account of the
other side of leadership -- solving problems in the world outside
the circle of the leader and his followers -- only insofar as it
shapes the tactics used to control followers.

Followers fall into two categories: mass and entourage.
The latter consists of those around the leader, variously called
his court, retinue or staff. They are the subordinates who
know him face-to-face. I will occasionally extend the term to
include senior subordinate leaders with whom the supreme leader
has a less intimate connection. My focus is upon the entourage
and little will be said about control over the mass, except where
comparison is appropriate.

There are three types of control. One is by a demonstration of virtue, which commands devotion[2] from the followers, who regard their service to the leader as a moral obligation, as an end in itself. The second motivation is what Barnard (1962:141) calls incentives; rewards (or punishments) which compensate for a lack of devotion. The third way is that of force; of particular interest is that variety of force which is called manipulation, the control of another person by devious methods.

My argument is as follows: In controlling an entourage the tactic of exciting devotion is used, but it has marked limitations. It is therefore necessary, in addition to devotion, to use either or both of the other tactics. I will ignore the <u>pure</u> use of incentives, on the grounds that it transforms a follower into an employee and therefore is not relevant to a discussion of leadership.[3] Instead I will attend to certain manipulative devices (including the use of incentives) which compensate for the inevitable shortcomings of the tactic of devotion.

It is essential to be clear about the nature of this argument. I begin with what leaders and others say about the way in which they behave towards the mass of their following and towards their retinues. From this behavior I deduce what must be the leader's ideas about human nature and human relationships. I am describing <u>their</u> cognitive maps. The argument goes only that far: whether human nature and human relationships are in fact like this, is another question.

Arousing Trust

First I will consider the strategy of arousing devotion, asking both why it is necessary and why it cannot be sufficient for the exercise of control over an entourage. The context is that of complex organizations; that is, large organizations like armies or governments or universities which are formally organized no bureaucratic principles.

The central problem of running a bureaucracy (or, for that matter, of applying a scientific theory in a practical world) is that both bureaucracy and science are based upon make-believe. This comes about because our capacity to separate things mentally, whether in analyzing the components of an existing whole or in designing a whole from hitherto unconnected mental elements, far exceeds our capacity to make such fission and fusion occur in nature. In other words, we can more easily make-believe that other things are equal than we can make them so. In a bureaucracy the dominating pretense is that men can be trained (in defined ranges of interaction) into bracketing away all of themselves except that part which makes them officials or clients. The metaphor is familiar but telling: the official and the client are "faceless." They are single roles: not that collection of roles that we call the person, still less the person with his passions and emotions, the personality. The principle of impersonal interaction leaves no room for devotion to a leader, but only to bureaucracy itself. To the former problem I will come shortly. I begin by describing various intrusions of the personal element which leaders make into the supposedly impersonal bureaucracy.

Churchill took a delight in writing memoranda to his staff usually containing sentences "with that prelude to preemptoriness 'Pray.'" Grigg, then (1942-1945) Secretary of State for War, remarks on the origins of these "prayers," listing "[Churchill's] own observations and imagination, paragraphs in newspapers and rumors from Fleet Street, the Smoking Room gossip, complaints or requests elicited by visits to factories, military and other units, or bombed cities" (1984:391). Before his elevation to ministerial level in 1942 Grigg had spent a lifetime as a Civil Servant and he remarks, when discussing the Churchillian prayers, that his own first rule of administration was not to keep dogs and still do his own barking. In these words, Grigg, as is proper in a Civil Servant, shows more faith in the imper-sonal monitoring and self-correcting devices built into the formal organization, than does Churchill. Churchill wants to see for himself, and in person, and happily pokes holes through the bureaucratic screen. True, some of the material comes from newspapers and from gossip and is therefore second-hand, nevertheless in all these endeavors Churchill is circumventing the "proper" channels of communication, and trying to see and hear things for himself. There was, as has often been re-marked, a quality of the *gamin* in Churchill, irreverence, mis-chief, a Street Arab's delight in popping up in unexpected places and causing consternation, and -- to judge, for example, from Alan Brooke's sentiments (Bryant, 1957:445) -- those involved, having (sometimes) chuckled, then got down to the serious business of getting the horse back in the stable before the escapade could have serious consequences. But Churchill was an unusual character and, as other cases will show, informal organization need have neither this element of irresponsibility nor the Churchillian randomness. Montgomery, one of Churchill's generals (and himself not without the quality of *gamin* -- or at least *enfant* *terrible*) went at the same task quite systematically.

Grigg (1948:422-24) gives a brief and interesting summary of Montgomery's techniques of leadership in the field and in battle. These techniques make it very clear that in Montgomery's reckoning -- but he did not so far as I know ever use such words -- the internal enemy was an excess of formal impersonal organization. In several different ways he elevated the person above and beyond the organization.

He kept a staff of liaison officers who spent their days at subordinate headquarters (down to divisional level or lower) returning nightly to report to Montgomery at Tactical H.Q. They were his "eyes and ears." They were also very often his mouth, for orders during battle went out directly and by the spoken word and not in writing. The liaison officer is clearly a device to improve the accuracy and speed of transmission both of information and of commands. But more is involved. The one-step transmission through a liaison officer is also a means of keeping vivid the image of the general's person and of putting the organization in the shadow.

Montgomery, as everyone knows, was anything but faceless. He strained to make himself easy to remember: the black beret with its two badges: the canaries in his map vehicle: his well-publicized habits of abstemiousness, early to bed, saying his prayers, all topped off with a conceit which at the time seemed vulgar beyond endurance (but far short of the heights more recently achieved by Idi Amin or Mohammed Ali the boxer) marked him out as more than just another general. It was consciously done, according to Grigg (1948:423): "He believed that if the Commander-in-Chief was a familiar figure to his men the more effect would his orders and messages have and the more readily would they react to his call for special efforts."

Before a campaign he made a practice of assemblying all the senior officers under his command and explaining to them what his intentions were and how the objectives would be accomplished. Notice that it is word of mouth again, not orders in writing; and those officers were required to go and deliver the message -- again in words -- to the officers and men of their own units. At the same time, Montgomery visited the different formations and gave the same message in addresses to mass audiences. To some extent, of course, all this activity is designed to transmit information: to see that the Eighth Army does not go off in the wrong direction or to ensure that the infantry does not attack until the artillery barrage has finished and paths have been cleared through the mine fields. But, it seems to a greater extent than conveying information, the purpose was to raise morale. The point is not merely that the soldier who does not know the reason why and has only the haziest idea of what to do (except die) is more likely to emulate good soldier Svejk than to be inspired by the troopers of the Light Brigade: the point rather is that, given face-to-face encounters, some of Montgomery's abundant confidence would rub off onto his men. According to Grigg, it indubitably did so; and -- amazingly -- within the three weeks that elapsed between his taking command and the first (defensive) battle of Alamein (1948:423). Even before the unbroken procession of victories began, his soldiers apparently trusted Montgomery.

One must resist the temptation to say that they had confidence in him as a man; or at least one must make clear the limitations of that phrase. What they saw, and what commanded their confidence, was not the man but an image shaped to excite the appropriate affect; a person in the original sense of per-sona, which is a "mask." This brings us to a problem. The rank and file and those in command of smaller formations are the mass in whom trust is to be aroused, and who must be brought to believe in the persona. But there are others -- the entour-age -- who are in a position to see behind the mask.

What of the senior officers who commanded larger units and those liaison officers who were part of Montgomery's entourage? The Montgomery known to them, while clearly less than the whole man, was presumably enough revealed to bring about that realism which borders on cynicism. Does it follow that a leader like Montgomery, by thrusting his face forward and emerging from the shadow of anonymity, thereby invites this nemesis?

That is exactly the price which such a leader must pay. Having elevated himself above the office and broken its confines, he has also lost its protection. The responsibility is his, and it is often proudly and boastfully undertaken: "The buck stops here." So does the blame: so does the possibility of sheltering behind an image. With the covering neither of an office nor of an image, how is a leader to protect himself from the cynical subordinate?

Again we make use of Grigg's commentary on Montgomery (1948:424). "He told me that he spent as much as a third of his time in choosing subordinates, going down as far as battalion commanders." Moreover he was "prone [to choose from] those whom he had himself commanded and observed in action."

Of course there were limits on his capacity to choose, some of them imposed by the rules of the formal organization. But, whatever these limits, Grigg's description speaks loudly to the incapacity of bureaucracy to cope with the complexity of human behavior. Advancement is not to be by seniority (an objective criterion) but by merit. Merit too can be objectified, as when recruitment or promotion is by examination. Even when there are too few positions to go round those qualified, objectivity can still be sustained by making the examinations competitive. But, as everyone knows, there is a difficulty: merit in the examina-tion room may turn out to be not the merit required on the job. Moreover, in the case of Montgomery and his officers in the field, an essential component in merit is trust. In fact, one must ascend even further into the heights of vagueness: per-sonal compatibility is a requirement. This means more than that the candidate subscribes to the ethos of the organization (hard-working, brave, honest and so forth): it means that he can get on with the people in the organization, in particular the leader, because he meets its informal requirements (he went to the right school, he speaks with the right accent, he knows the right people, or whatever else). I have used the caricature of the English upper classes and the public school "old boy" network: but it happens everywhere in formal organizations and without it they work less well (Barnard, 1962:224).

Why did Montgomery make his own choices and why was he not content to let the organization do it for him? The answer is obvious, but also somewhat startling. He wanted to replicate himself: he wanted people down there who would act as he himself would act in their place. They must be trustworthy. It is not just the crude reckoning that they owe their advancement to him and that he can as easily break them. It is more than that they are loyal to him. It is not even that they know him and would therefore "react more readily to his call for special efforts" (Grigg, 1948:423). Rather, in that highly personal selection, they become part of his "household," even part of him: any contractual component in the relationship is thereby surpressed. That is conveyed by the patriarchal metaphor: Montgomery's liaison officers and personally appointed subordinates were part of his "household." You are likely both to love and hate a patriarch: but you do not have a contract with him, and he is more than just a means of getting some task accomplished.

We now have an interim conclusion. For purely instrumental reasons, a leader must make use of informal organization, of personal ties, of devotion, and therefore of effect. The job which he must do exceeds the capacity of any formal organization and calls for the use of emotions.

But there are difficulties. The passions -- whether positive or negative -- seem constantly to demand for themselves an intrinsic status. Such relationships become ends in themselves, no longer a means for acting upon the world outside the relationships. Insofar as they achieve an intrinsic status, and deny their own instrumentality, they also deny the task. Nehru's loyalty to his second-rate entourage and the resulting inefficiencies (Brecher, 1959:168ff.) offer an example. In short, while leadership can only be achieved in the context of a formal organization by the use of informal organization (which is the use of personal ties and therefore of emotion), the emotion must be kept under control. One way of doing this is to balance one element with its opposite: to foster an instrumental outlook by creating uncertainty, which is our next topic. In the present discussion, too, we have described a strategy of contraries: augmenting and softening the pure instrumenality of a formal organization by creating trust.

Exciting Uncertainty

I have argued that a leader needs to arouse devotion, but that to do so brings its own dangers. I now go back to that state of affairs which makes it hard for him to command respect from his entourage, let alone their devotion.

My starting proposition is this: the more frequent and the more intense the interaction between the leader and follower, the more likely is the relationship to be "in the round" -- what Gluckman called "multiplex" (1955:19) -- and the harder it becomes for the leader to keep up his halo and to appear to be virtuous. Frequency and multiplicity characterize relationships between a leader and his entourage. In such conditions, the principle strategy for controlling the entourage is the creation not only of trust (already discussed), but also of its contrary: uncertainty. For a variety of reasons it can pay the leader (up to a point) to keep the world of his immediate subordinates (but not of his mass following) fragmented and at the fringe of their comprehension.

Here, first, is an extreme example, reported by Fynn, a visitor to the court of Shaka Zulu (Walter, 1969:134).

> Cattle and war formed the whole subject of his conversations; and during his sitting, while in the act of taking a pinch of snuff, or when engaged in the deepest conversation, he would by a movement of his finger, perceivable only by his attendants, point out one of the gathering sitting around him, upon which ... the man would be carried off and killed. This was a daily occurrence. On one occasion 60 boys under twelve years of age were dispatched before he had breakfasted. No sooner is the signal given, and the object pointed out, than those sitting around him scramble to kill him, although they have good reason to expect the next moment the same fate themselves, but such apprehensions are far from their thoughts; the will of the King being uppermost.
>
> I have seen instances where they have had opportunities of speaking while being carried off, but which they always employed in enthusiastically praising the heroic deeds of their king.

These could be acts of self indulgence by a despot who was psychotic. Gluckman, indeed, argued (1960:168) that Shaka was "at least a latent homosexual and possibly psychotic." Walter replies, reasonably enough, that these acts can be shown to be, no less plausibly, "a product of calculation" (1969:148). For my purpose the psychological explanation is irrelevant (whether or not true), because my interest is not in motivations but in the effect of such horrendous behavior. The effect was to create uncertainty. What Shaka did was predictable insofar as the entourage knew that from time to time someone's neck was going to be broken, but they did not know whose it would be nor were they given any explanation for the deed.

There are some less spectacular examples. Frank Moraes (1973:245) produced the following wry vignette of Indira Gandhi:

Mrs. Gandhi has the reputation of never forgetting. More ominously, she rarely forgives. She has shown a capacity for toppling restive colleagues as deftly as she has toppled a good few inconvenient State governments. Watching her in action today, surrounded by her courtier-ministers, all conscious that at any moment the axe may descend on their necks, one wonders whether a male liberation movement is not overdue in India, or in Asia.

The morale and self confidence of the entourage may be lessened without ever letting the axe fall on their necks. Franklin Roosevelt delegated authority with just this effect. The divisions of responsibility were imprecise so that a subordinate could never be sure whether he or someone else was charged with a particular task. Roosevelt would also put together, to work   in the same agency or even at the same job, men whose points of view and whose personalities were antagonistic, thus exciting conflict (Burns, 1956:370-375). To say the least, this does not seem to be the most rational way to bring about the efficient implementation of policies.

Nor does Governor Jerry Brown emerge as the model of the rational and predictable leader. The following quotation comes from Time 1976:

> Brown trusts few aides, often delegates by default, concentrates on the flap of the moment, and ignores matters lacking crisis or deadline pressure explaining 'the yeast hasn't risen yet.'

The then Senator Deukmejian said: "He's so inconsistent, and many people feel that he does it deliberately and shrewdly. You never really know where he's coming from." As Brown himself affirmed: "A little vagueness goes a long way in this business."

In fact, it is difficult to find a leader who is not, at least on some occasions, an irritant for those who surround him. It is hard to find even someone with the usual array of social graces (Franklin Roosevelt is an exception). Eisenhower, almost alone, stands out as non-threatening, a good mixer, a nice man to have around. Gandhi was certainly a strain.

We have a range of negative qualities: vicious, irascible, provoking discord, unlovable, aloof, erratic, eccentric, unreasonable, at the very least a source of discomfort. Most of this, it is to be noted, is the very opposite of what is conveyed in the image put out for the mass of followers. How is such behavior towards the entourage to be explained?

First the milder negative qualities, such as being reserved or aloof, may be allowed to spill over into the public image and they have some obvious positive consequences. Alan Brooke, according to Montgomery (1961:123) "is not an easy person to get to know well, and he gives the impression to some that he is cold and 'distant,' and perhaps a bit callous." Lord Nuffield (Montgomery, 1961:154) is "shy and doesn't like meeting people." Nehru was "moody, lonely, vain, proud and reserved" (Brecher, 1959:608). Coolidge, admittedly a less than forceful leader, was, on social occasions, taciturn, acerbic and abrupt (Barber in Paige, 1972:90). Many leaders, in short, turn out to be less than charming in personal interactions, and in this way they preserve a mystique: the image that their mind is always on higher things and that their responsibilities leave no room for social graces. Carried over from social occasions to interactions with the entourage, this style is a hedge against the risk of excessive familiarity. Marginality, in fact, is a characteristic of leaders. Some, like Hitler, boast of their unpromising origins -- "a man without a name, without money, without influence..." (Fest, 1974:521). Indeed, a generalized marginality is a necessity. Leaders must avoid continuing identification with any particular group so that they can be seen to represent the whole. They must also separate themselves from the whole, on pain of losing their distinction. In short, a measure of unpleasantness provides a necessary distance.

For the more severely negative traits, however, that is not a satisfactory explanation. The devices seem too extreme to make sense, if they are no more than a way of choking off familiarity. What other consequences might be intended?

A second explanation is that it is rational to incite anger and discord among one's staff, because in that way they are tricked, like unwary card players, into revealing their hands. They are provoked into saying what they feel and think. Churchill "would make some quite outrageous statements to the Chiefs of Staff, just to arouse their heated opposition and get their real views" (Montgomery, 1961:119). Moreover there are times when it pays to break down inhibitions and to goad people out of their timidity. Burns argues convincingly (1956:371ff.) that by his techniques of "fuzzy delegation" and pitting one advisor against another and so stirring up a welter of conflicting opinions, Roosevelt was doing exactly what was needed to stimulate the "freshness and vitality" required to implement the New Deal.

Third, uncertainty may generate frantic action. The staff members endeavor, by intensifying their efforts, to anticipate every contingency. Not knowing what the leader wants, they try to anticipate his every desire, and to fulfill them all; which is, of course, an impossibility. Short of the level of frantic action, uncertainty at least serves to keep the entourage on its toes. In the administrative world, this is the purpose of surprise inspections.

This suggests that the creation of uncertainty has in it an element of training. In fact more is involved than simple administrative devices like the surprise inspection. We have arrived at a fact which ultimately shapes the relationship between a leader and his entourage: that together they have the task of dealing with the real world. The real world is not that simplified and purified image which is conveyed to the masses. It is a world of failures, a world often too complicated for rational management, a world of frustrated hopes and failures, where the most important lesson to be learned is to know that things will go wrong and that the only real failure is the failure to pick oneself up, work out what went wrong, and try again. In other words, the more effective subordinate is the one who can cope with disappointments and with pressure. (This is, of course, as true for the leaders as it is for their subordinates.)

But this explanation of why leaders behave towards their immediate staff in ways that are vicious, erratic, eccentric, and unreasonable, still is not enough. The behavior also has a fourth effect, one already noticed. A leader's hostile manipulations put a strain upon whatever devotion the members of the entourage feel towards him. Someone who is irascible, unreasonable, unpredictable and vicious, is that much the harder to love and respect. The devotion, if it is sustained, must come from a deep well; alternatively the leader has countervailing qualities. But notice that as soon as one talks of a balancing act between good and bad qualities, one approaches a world of accounting and calculation, and the moral relationship of devotion shades into instrumentality. In short, whenever the members of an entourage see themselves as being treated unreasonably or unfairly by their leader, they are thereby induced to see the relationship with him as instrumental. The more he behaves in this way, the more he foregoes his chances of commanding devotion from members of the entourage. But in fact a leader has no alternative because there are limits to devotion, and when it fails as a mechanism of control, the method of uncertainty must be employed.

My fifth explanation picks up a theme which underlies its four predecessors. It concerns not expected consequences but rather a leader's conception of his relationship with his entourage. I will argue that there is an inevitable element of hostility in this relationship.

To treat followers without consideration, to make them feel anxious and insecure or even merely uncomfortable, could be a signal that they are of small importance and an indication that they play an insignificant part in one's scheme of things. There is, in the otherwise urbane Davies, a strangely vituperative passage on those whom he calls "staff" (1963:284-285). "They want to be like the boss but unlike his followers." They want to share power "without undertaking the arduous and dangerous task of acquiring it." He refers to "the impotence of staff members" who must use "cunning" to gain their way, and concludes they "can only pretend to eminence." These are presented as objective facts, but they sound more like something said by an embittered leader. In any case the evident contempt is perfectly consistent with the overweening behavior that I have described.

A studied unconcern for dignity of one's entourage may in fact be a manipulative tactic and a sign of exactly the opposite of unconcern: that person is treated with ostensible lack of consideration because he is dangerous. That will be my argument. The behavior of leaders towards their entourage can only indicate that they see members of this entourage as a threat to themselves; to their policies, to their dominance, and to the maintenance of the image of the leader before the masses. The leader sees them in the way that a despot sees his subjects, a necessary but also destructive force that needs constant stimulation and containment. Leadership is evidently an enterprise that requires some degree of precautionary paranoia.

Sometimes this "paranoia" may be justified. A leader who attempts to innovate may find himself opposed by conservative persons in his entourage. The entourage may have been visited upon him ex officio as in the case of a permanent Civil Service (the continuing altercations between the British Treasury officials and various Labor Governments are examples). Alternatively, as in Shaka's case, the opposition may come from an elite surviving from an earlier regime. Labour Ministers no doubt did the best they could and much depended on the personalities of the Minister and the official. Shaka had a shorter way, as might be expected.

> The elders, as in any traditional society, not only served as the living archives of custom and law, but also exerted moral influence on the ruler ... not only participating in important decisions, but also exercising restraint in various ways on the power of the ruler. Any innovating chief or king who seeks to rule without traditional limitations must deal with the resistance of the elders.

> Shaka dealt with this resistance by redefining the status of the old men and then slaughtering them. Instead of respected persons who had passed from active service to venerable authority, they were declared to be useless "old women" who were unfit for fighting. It appears that before their extermination, Shaka had changed their status by instituted ridicule. It is said that he had compelled them to wear petticoats of monkey skins, shaped like the garments of old women, for battle dress... Around the time the Ndwandwe were defeated, he gathered the aged men and had them killed. Even if some were spared, it is

clear that their power as a group was ended and that those who survived were prevented by terror from attempting to influence the King. (Walter, 1969: 164-164)

No one need be surprised when a leader removes those who oppose his policies, when he has the power to do so. It is a perfectly rational act. It is not so easy to accept as invariably rational the kind of paranoia which insists that subordinates are disposed towards treachery. Rational or not, the theme is very common and takes several forms. The leader is betrayed by his lieutenants (Hobsbawm, 1959:14-15). The divine king, his powers waning, must by an act of duty kill himself or be slaughtered by his own closest advisors (Evans-Pritchard, 1962:ch. iv and Krige, E. J. and J. D., 1943:ch 10).

Shaka saw himself beset with this danger and had several ways of meeting it, one of which will come as no surprise. Shaka's entourage was made up of the amaphakathi.

These amaphakathi, literally meaning the members of the inner circle, often surrounded him in the royal kraal and accompanied him on marches. In many respects they were similar to what the Romans had called comites -- namely, officers, companions, and attendants making up a retinue. Some were izinduna, ministers chosen by the despot, whose personal loyalty had rewarded them with office and whose power and survival depended entirely on him. Others were the heads of chiefdoms and lineages formerly independent, whose original authority had not been created by the despot but who now gave him fealty and attended his presence. In addition, the generals were among the most important members of the circle. (Walter, 1969: 165)

Later we read

He killed chiefs and other important persons whose loyalty he suspected and replaced them with kinsmen and other favorites. Throughout his reign, suspicion was enough to cause the violent removal of any lieutenant, and getting the despot's ear to plant suspicions was an important move to be made in the complex intrigues of the inner circle. Ferguson believed that there were indications that Shaka lived in fear of his several induna. Certainly, the pattern of violence that ravaged the circle around the despot in great assemblies had [a] terroristic effect on the amaphakathi. (Walter, 1969:166).

There are less sanguinary ways, ones less expensive of human talent, to keep in check the supposed ambitions of subordinates. One reads, almost with a sense of relief, that Shaka also ruled by dividing, setting one subordinate against another. The retinue -- amaphakathi -- were required not only to implement decisions but also to give the despot advice on matters of public importance. He took care, however, to ensure that this advice never came from the whole body, but only from sections of it, and he played favorites between the sections, according to the enthusiasm with which they accepted his opinion. In this way the council was never in a position to unite against him (Walter, 1969:165-166). In essence, Franklin Roosevelt was making use of a similar tactic, when he placed incompatible subordinates together in the same agency, and when, by leaving vague the limits of their jurisdictions, he made it likely that they would squabble (Burns, 1956:371). Elsewhere Burns (1956:151), having described the cacophony of advice which Roosevelt solicited, remarks: "Clearly [he] was not disposed to establish a powerful chief of staff or dominating idea man in the White House."

There is an obvious way to counter the changes of treacherous subordinates, but it causes problems: to choose second rate people. Those years in India of murmuring "After Nehru, who?" reflect not only his towering status, but also the low quality of his entourage. He was, as Brecher argues (1959:628), a poor "judge of character" and a man of such intense loyalty that he kept around him old comrades who had proven themselves incompetent and sometimes dishonest. Brecher goes on to say (1959:631ff.) that Nehru was not, as many people thought, "indifferent to the succession problem," but rather believed that the Indian people, appreciating his socialist policies, would insist that the Congress party find an appropriate successor. Whatever the motives -- loyalty to old friends, mistrust of right wing tendencies in the Congress, or faith in the people's wisdom -- the result was that there was no cadre of able younger men around Nehru, from among whom his successor might have been chosen. The result of that was an unchallenged eminence for the leader (whether he thought that way or not) because the young and the ambitious and the able were not brought forward.

The suggestion that leaders think along these paranoid lines is supported by the different way in in which they manipulate different categories of subordinate, the specialists and the generalists. The specialists are experts who provide advice on defined topics or carry out defined tasks. Churchill, the statesman, had an unfortunate habit of trying to interfere directly in the military conduct of the war. "The sparks used to fly quite a lot in Whitehall ...," Montgomery reports (1961:112). Sometimes Montgomery became involved but, being in the field "...I couldn't be sent for to No. 10. I could, of course, have been sacked, but so long as we won our battles that was unlikely."

Montgomery is correct. But there is more to be said. He was spared the irritations suffered by Churchill's immediate entourage not only because he was in North Africa or across the Channel, but also because he was an expert, having, compared to Churchill, a relatively narrow range of responsibility. He was not (despite his inclinations) a statesman. The expert is less subjected to manipulation (and within the field of his own expertise more resistant to it) than is the subordinate who is a generalist, because the expert is not a rival and a potential usurper. The generalists -- those eminent enough -- are the leaders' "look-alikes" and threaten him with replacement. It is for his reason that in the traditional kingdoms of India the administrators came not from the ruler's caste but from the caste of Brahmans, who were ritually barred from the kingship. Shaka was wary of his royal brothers and it was a rule that the "great induna" (prime minister) was "never a member of the royal family" (Gluckman, 1940:33). Characteristically Shaka lessened the "look-alike" threat, when he gained power, by exterminating many of his close relatives and (Walter, 1969:163) even refusing "to marry or beget heirs." When one concubine did produce an infant, he killed it with his own hands and had the mother put to death. In less violent cultures, it is not unknown for a leader to remove the threat of a too-eminent subordinate by transforming him into a specialist and charging him with a task at which he is sure to fail and so fall from his eminence.

Repression is clearly not the only form of manipulation. None but the very peculiar would voluntarily take up a position which offered only penalties. The leader depends upon his entourage to make his leadership a success, both by carrying out his decisions and by helping to create and preserve the image by which he attains legitimacy and devotion among the masses. So there are rewards. The entourage, like the donkey, is controlled by the carrot and the stick, but not quite in the same way: the stick is held in front of its members, to prevent them from advancing to the point where the leader's own position might be in jeopardy.

The argument thus has led from devotion, a moral relationship, to its negative image: enmity between the leader and his entourage. How does this progression come about and how is it checked?

The Controlling Circumstances

Neither in Grigg's (1948:422-24) brief discussion of Montgomery's techniques of leadership nor in a somewhat more ample description (Bryant, 1957) of Montgomery (and Alan Brooke) commanding in the disastrous campaigns in 1940, is there the slightest hint that they ever deliberately excited uncertainty among their staff. On the contrary, they -- Montgomery in particular -- were a source of confidence and strength in circumstances which could hardly have been more confusing and demoralizing. It seems, perhaps, ingenuous to put the obvious question and give the obvious answer. Churchill, deliberating on higher strategy, could afford to irritate and confuse, because there was time for deliberation and in any case the course of action had not been settled and, most important, circumstances did not dictate what must be done. Still more could Roosevelt, in crises certainly but not yet at war, afford to play the manipulative games that served to educate, control and goad his entourage. But for the general in the field, and in a way of movement (such as the retreat before Dunkirk), there is not the time to think about training or educating subordinates. By then it is too late. The situation is dominated, in other words, by the external task: in this case to win (or least not to lose) the battle, and battles are more quickly lost when subordinate commanders pit their energies against each other rather than against the enemy.[4]

That is obvious enough. But the salience of the task has one important effect which is not so obvious. Think of the noun "politics." In contemporary English usage there is one meaning of the word which is derogatory, referring to those manipulations and intrigues by which a leader assembles or controls a following, by implication doing so to the detriment of the general interest. If he serves the general interest he is not "playing politics" but rather is being "statesmenlike." This is nothing more than a re-statement of what has just been said about "tasks," and it rests upon the distinction between the two faces of leadership: that directed internally on the leader and his group and that directed externally for action upon the world.

A leader and his entourage must both be in touch with reality -- that is, with the world outside their own interactions. They cannot afford to close their eyes and to conceal difficulties and failures and inadequacies, as may be done in the making of an image for the masses.

The members of the entourage should possess certain qualities which make them better able to deal with reality. One of these qualities is the possession of that kind of muscular personality which shows itself as ambition. They must be capable of exercising initiative, and an entourage entirely devoid of initiative and ambition would be of use to a leader only as looking glass in which to indulge his vanity. At least on the evidence presented it seems clear that leaders believe that the members of their retinue have ambitions, which must be tickled and rewarded and played off against one another and ultimately stifled.

A linked quality required in the entourage is intelligence and the capacity to doubt and to ask questions. This quality is in complementary distribution with devotion. To be intelligent and to ask questions and to express doubt falls short of cynicism, but it is a step on the same road: and cynicism is an arsenic for devotion. Conversely, devotion poisons intelligence and inhibits rationality -- that is to say, it blinds one to realities and it stifles questioning.

We come back again to the controlling circumstance: the leader and his entourage rub against reality. Reality, if the wrong decisions are taken, produces disappointments and failures. So far as is possible, the bad news must not be allowed to darken the image which goes out to the masses: or, if the disaster is of such magnitude that it cannot be concealed, then various secondary devices are employed to protect the leader from blame.[5] But the entourage is in a different position. Not only do they come to know the facts about what went wrong, and not only do they know how far the leader is responsible, but they are also required to think about these events and to try to make sure that matters will be conducted differently in the future. The entourage must be seen as a threat, because they know too much.

Since there are tasks to be done, a leader needs the services of his retinue. Since both the leader and the retinue are at work in the real world of performance (and not merely the world of images) they have frequent experience of failures and inadequacies. In this world the myth-making which might serve as the basis for pure devotion as to a god is an impossibility. Devotion to the person is a possibility, but that, taken too far, gets in the way of efficiency. The alternative to devotion is an instrumental relationship, which is characterized by accounting, rewards, punishments and manipulation. Here too excess is penalized because neither the leader nor his entourage have time or energy left to deal with problems outside the circle of their own interactions.

To conclude. I have described several ways in which effective leaders behave disruptively. They upset bureaucratic orderliness by injecting themselves as persons (not as officials), by stirring up conflicts between those who should be cooperating, by promoting uncertainty and -- the biggest paradox -- by treating some of their followers as if they were enemies. Without a doubt they break the rules.

But in practice the potential descent into chaos is arrested by a set of meta-rules which regulate the breaking of ordinary rules. These meta-rules have more in common with the automatic compensatory mechanisms of a marketplace than with customary rules. Over-reliance on formal organization is penalized by inefficiency -- that is, by a failure to perform tasks and ultimately by the loss of power. Personal interactions (moral relationships) compensate, but taken too far they encounter the same penalty. The remedy is manipulation (instrumental relationships), but if that is carried to excess, the result again is failure.

To conclude, it seems that an essential component in the art of leadership is balancing contraries. But "balancing" has the wrong connotations. It suggests a continuing restraint, stopping processes well short of the point of collapse, an avoidance of risk, a curtailing of energy, mediation, the medium and, therefore in the end, mediocrity. Of course there are in practice mediocre leaders, and there will sometimes be situations which make sensible a resolute cleaving to the middle way, but the idea of leadership is certainly the very antithesis of mediocrity. So also, I believe more often than not, is the practice of leadership. The art is not that of keeping the pendulum near to rest in the center, but rather one should emulate the child on a swing: the higher the better, short of tumbling off.

With such complexity, it is not surprising that if management has become a science, leadership is still an art.

NOTES

[1]The foundation (for my analysis) is Raymond Firth's (1961) critical commentary on the structural-functionalist studies of some of his contemporaries. Briefly, he argued that their generalizations in the form of principles (for example, sibling solidarity) or even of rules (mother's brother gives a cow to sister's son) left much behavior unconsidered and therefore unexplained, because it pushed towards the general rather than towards the specific. If one moves downwards towards behavior one enters a world of "making do with what is available" (the pragmatic rather than the normative, to use a not very successful distinction I essayed in 1969). One is then left with the normative not so much as a guide for action, but rather both as a repertoire for justification and accusation, and as a simplifying facade which makes the world appear less complicated than we know it to be: in other words, Ibsen's "life's lie." Thus there is a part of culture that is relatively overt and another that is relatively covert, and my interest has been to search for regularities and patterns in the covert sector. I have done this in the context of university life and committee behavior (1977) and, more generally, by investigating the way in which displays of emotion can be used to control or stimulate others (n.d.). The present enquiry is into the dark half of leadership.

[2]The devotion may be to the leader as a person (charismatic) or it may be to him as the representative or embodiment of a cause or a tradition. In the latter case, the devotion is tempered by accountability, since the leader does not have the status of being an end in himself. In practice devotion is always a mixture of these things and its precise composition has important tactical consequences for the control of followers. The subject is too large for proper discussion here, but, briefly, I think that, other things being equal, the greater the charisma, the greater the likelihood of a disruptive style of leadership.

[3]In the same way it might be argued that the pure use of force, with no element of persuasion whatsoever, does not constitute leadership. The slave has a master, not a leader.

[4]Compare Fest (1974:674-5) writing on Hitler:

> The principal of rival authorities [...] was scarcely appropriate for the struggle against a resolute

enemy, [...] It finally led to a condition approaching total anarchy.

and

Rational classifications, structural arrangements, any kind of quiet authority, were fundamentally so alien to him that until literally the last day of the war he repeatedly encouraged his entourage to feud over positions, competences, and ridiculous questions of rank.

[5]One of the many paradoxes of this strange relationship is that the entourage constitutes a protection for the leader's infallibility. This does not mean that they always give him good advice, but rather that when things go wrong, they must take the blame. This is the traditional role of the adjutant in a regiment. He accepts responsibility for things administratively mishandled: but, when all goes well, it is owing to the genius of the colonel.

REFERENCES

Bailey, F. G., 1969. Stratagems and Spoils, Oxford: Blackwell.

Bailey, F. G., 1977. Morality and Expediency, Oxford: Blackwell.

Bailey, F. G., n.d. The Tactical Uses of Passion, Ithaca, New York: Cornell University Press (forthcoming).

Barnard, C. I., 1962 [1938]. The Functions of the Executive, Cambridge: Harvard University Press.

Brecher, Michael, 1959. Nehru: A Political Biography, London: Oxford University Press.

Bryant, Arthur, 1957. The Turn of the Tide: 1939-1943, London: Collins.

Burns, James MacGregor, 1956. Roosevelt: The Lion and the Fox, New York: Harcourt, Brace, Jovanovich.

Davies, James C., 1963. Human Nature in Politics, New York: Wiley.

Evans-Pritchard, E. E., 1962. Essays in Social Anthropology, London: Faber and Faber.

Fest, Joachim C., 1975. Hitler, New York: Random House.

Firth, Raymond, 1961. Elements of Social Organization, London: Watts.

Gluckman, Max, 1940. "The Kingdom of the Zulu" in African Political Systems, Fortes, M. and Evans-Pritchard, E. E. (eds.), London: Oxford University Press.

Gluckman, Max, 1955. The Judicial Process Among the Barotse of Northern Rhodesia, Manchester: Manchester University Press.

Gluckman, Max, 1960. "The Rise of the Zulu Empire," Scientific American, Vol. 202, 1960, pp. 157-168.

Grigg, P. J., 1948. Prejudice and Judgement, London: Jonathan Cap.

Hobsbawm, E. J., 1959. Primitive Rebels, Manchester: Manchester University Press.

Krige, E. Jensen and J. D., 1943. The Realm of the Rain Queen, London: Oxford University Press.

Montgomery, of Alamein, 1961. The Path to Leadership, London: Collins.

Moraes, Frank, 1973. Witness to an Era: India 2910 to the Present Day, New York: Holt, Rinehart and Winston.

Paige, Glenn D. (ed.), 1972. Political Leadership: Readings for an Emerging Field, New York: The Free Press.

Walter, E. V., 1960. Terror and Resistance, New York: Oxford University Press.

Session Two

Discussion

BAILEY: My paper narrows the issue under discussion to micro-politics, a level not without moral concerns. The most useful thing I can do here is to set my essay in a series of contexts: (1) the context of my own prejudices, (2) the context of the anthropological framework in which I am working, particularly the notion of how one treats the idea of culture, and (3) the context of the other essays presented at this conference. The first two contexts I can be quite brief about, the third will occupy most of my time.

As for my own prejudices, I am going to mention only two. One is not entirely serious, but it is certainly part of the motivation. I adopt a view of leaders from underneath: I am interested primarily in their failings, their weaknesses, how they can be defeated. And if I have a hero in this effort, it is not, as some of my colleague keep telling me, that I have been keeping Machiavelli's Prince under the pillow too long. Not at all. The other prejudice I think is more serious. It has to do with my ideas about culture which I shall characterize below. I believe quite profoundly that full rationality, the full use of reason, is an impossibility in the art of government. Nevertheless it is absolutely necessary to strive continually to achieve such rationality.

This leads to the second context, the general anthropological framework in which I am working, and the particular notion of culture that I accept. Culture in the anthropological sense is a set of ideas and values which we use to understand the world, and to attempt to guide our behavior. It helps us understand other people's behavior, and the things we see around us. This culture is emphatically a thing of reason. It has to assume that we can operate on the world with some degree of success, that there is a connection between means and ends, and that some of the time our ends are achieved. However, very often we do not achieve the ends we have set for ourselves. And thus culture may be a screen which entirely obscures our vision of reality, yet which is absolutely necessary in order for us to be in touch with reality at all. Sometimes our vision and our ideas are tested by experience because the actions that we put into practice produce a result that we did not expect. This is an important point. Sometimes we modify our views, our culture, in light of that experience, but very often we do not. We elaborate some secondary explanation to tell us that the world, despite our experience, is still the way we thought it was. That I think is the essence of religion. It is also the essence of ideologies and one of the sources of irrationality in politics.

76

I will spend the remainder of my time on the third context, the inquiry that surrounds the paper: I am interested in the culture of leadership. Although I use historical material and materials from novels, biographies, and other sources, I do not pretend to be writing about Churchill or Roosevelt or somebody else. By the culture of leadership I mean a set of ideas and a set of values which concern the exercise of power in a particular culture. The last phrase, "in a particular culture," is important. In different contexts and in different cultures we find different sets of ideas and different kinds of explanations for exercising power. I found it quite impossible to work with leadership on this extraordinary general level. So quite arbitrarily I narrowed my inquiry to what my reading and interests dictated: the question of how a leader controls his followers. Obviously controlling followers is not the only thing that leaders do. They also interact with other leaders, allies, and enemies, but my concentration is entirely on the followers. The phenomenon to be explained is the range of tactics or strategies available to leaders for the control of their followers.

Even this is an extraordinarily large and variegated complex, and a difficult topic to address. And thus in the process of doing this exercise I made the following kinds of divisions. First of all, the tactics and the strategies available in a particular culture will vary with how that culture defines "followers." The culture from which I am drawing most but not all of my materials is that of statesmen and politicians -- Churchill, Roosevelt, military leaders and others. And in these the first clear division, it seemed to me, was between the mass and the "entourage," or what other people call "the staff." The second area involves cultural and historical variations and constraints; I will expand on these later in the paper and here when I discuss types of followers. The third and most important factor is the particular situation, the particular problem with which the leader is dealing at that time.

I think it is sufficient at this stage to deal with just three main strategies available to leaders for the control of their followers. The first strategy I call the demotic style of leadership. This strategy characterizes a wide range of leaders. It could refer, for example, to the type of leader who says, "Come on you guys, let's go, let's go, let's go," and waits until everybody gets up and says, "yes, let's go, let's go, let's go," and off they go. This style of leadership is not uniquely American. I have watched Indian villagers behaving in exactly that kind of way on informal occasions when they go out hunting. This is the way they make a decision to move from one stand to the next when they hunt. On other occasions, in the formal setting of the village, the leader becomes an autocrat.

The second strategy or style of leadership is designated by the Latin word "numen." Its' root meaning is "to nod," and then it comes to mean assent, extensionally a divinity, a god, a person who makes the decisions, who is remote, removed, who is not to be questioned, whose actions are such that you must not seek justification, you simply obey.

The demotic and numen styles can be combined in various mixtures. Charles de Gaulle, for example, could be quite remote and aloof, and yet he was sometimes quite demotic. I refer here not only to the famous gesture of exhibiting invulnerability by shaking hands in the middle of hostile crowds, but also to some of the things that he said: a typical demotic pattern is to shed the culture of a leader and speak like the common people. The master of this was Joey Smallwood in Newfoundland who exhibited the demotic style par excellence.

The third strategy or style of leadership involves presenting oneself as the representative of a cause of some kind. A cause is assumed by the followers to have an intrinsic value; they attribute this value to the leader who is seen to exemplify this cause.

All three strategies have their strengths and weaknesses. The demotic style has a very clear weakness: if the leader becomes too much of a buddy he ceases to be an effective leader. We find many examples of leaders who overreach themselves in this way. The weakness of the third strategy is also fairly obvious. The leader is held accountable. If he fails in the eyes of his followers to represent the cause, he becomes dispensable. This is not true of the charismatic leader. The charismatic leader's power resides in himself, not in what he represents. The essence of all three strategies is that they allow for a vast amount of "deceit." (I suppose that is the word.) If a leader can present an image that is far removed from reality and thus from accountability, the followers will have difficulty in understanding, in asking questions, and will also have difficulty in freeing themselves and being out of control.

There is another level at which the followers may be considered. This level concerns the dispositions among these people, whether followers or entourage, and I still have to work out how to separate such dispositions. The dispositions seem to fall very nicely on a scale, and there are four elements in this scale. At one extreme is the follower who is characterized by the splendid phrase, "the failure of nerve." We touched on this issue earlier when we discussed the conditions in which people are disposed to accept a charismatic leader. This is the situation in which things have fallen apart, in which the merits or the rewards that people get are not seen to be in proportion to the merits or to the efforts they put in. In other words, it is a world where the culture as a guide has failed to allow people to make sense of what is happening. That is the occasion for the rise, the emergence of a particular leader; I am going to call him charismatic.

This is one situation. The next one along the line is the "regimented follower." I mean by regimented follower typically the regular soldier, the person who does what he is told and no more, who does not ask questions, who acts more or less automatically, who does not have a mind of his own. There is more to be said but let me move quickly on to the next one -- the mature follower. The mature follower is the one who anticipates what the leader wants and will do it without being told, who is ready to offer suggestions and even to ask for justification and to offer criticism. In certain contexts this is the ideal type of follower, just as in other contexts the regimented one is the ideal type of follower. In no context is the loss-of-nerve person the ideal follower.

Now to move to the final fourth one. This is the anarchic follower, the one in whom the capacity to act without guidance has moved beyond that, to a refusal to wait for guidance and an insistence on doing it for himself. That man is, in the quite literal sense, no longer a follower. Those are the dispositions of the followers.

I will now consider briefly other contexts which would reshape the arguments of my essay. One of the institutional contexts of leadership appears clearly if the leader holds an established office that sets constraints upon what he may do, and also gives him resources for controlling the followers. There is a much wider set of contexts that can also be taken into account. By wider I mean, for example, that the leader-follower interaction in the world or politics is not the same as in the world of religion. Gandhi is a wonderful case in this respect. We heard earlier about Gandhi's leadership; to understand this we have to understand that Gandhi exemplified an approved style of life and thus defined a particular kind of person within a particular culture.

This leads us to a general point that ought to be made about all these contexts, including even the institutional one. Contexts are not simply given as constraints; they are, I think, manipulatable, changeable, redefinable; if the leader is astute, he is able to do so. Gandhi again is a case in point. Gandhi presented himself as the saint of the Hindu, the man detached from life. But the values that Gandhi preached were oddly enough in many respects not Hindu at all. They were values not of renunciation, but of activity, they were values that concerned the moral worth of individuals in this life and not what would happen to you in the next life. There are thus a variety of other things that forced Gandhi and other leaders, who have to use a cultural context, to walk a tightrope. A leader does not simply accept the cultural condition in which he is placed. This cultural condition is there to be manipulated. Or to put it another way, followers must be educated to see that their culture is perhaps not the most appropriate one or the best one.

Finally, there is the context that I am calling situation. What I mean simply is that we do not understand the choice or the range of strategies and tactics open to a particular leader unless we also understand how the leader himself and his followers see the problem that is before them.

A few concluding general remarks. I want to emphasize that in my essay, and indeed in everything else that I am going to write on this topic, I attempt not to be prescriptive in the moral sense. I do not know what the good leader is anymore than I know what the good life is. I have a much more limited aim than that. The first is, I have to say what the particular goal is that I am interested in, and I told you that it is in controlling followers. What I then do is survey the strategies that are available in a particular culture and eventually in several societies for purposes of comparison. Then the third level of explanation is to say under what conditions, in what context, is one strategy more appropriate and effective than the other to achieve a particular goal.

CLAUDE: We have become increasingly aware that the requirements for effective and successful leadership are variable. These requirements certainly vary according to place. No one ought to expect that the same qualities that make for effective leadership in the United States would make for effective leadership in China or India or some other culture or setting. They vary in time. There is very probably a difference between the qualities of leadership in the 18th century and in the late 20th century, for instance. And they must surely vary according to context. It makes a difference whether we are talking about politics or medicine or art or religion or whatever. And thus it seems to me clear that the field of leadership may need less generalization than distinction-making and particularization.

I recall the discussion among students of international organization about the nature of the leadership of the secretary general of an international organization. We tend to rely on two models: Sir Eric Drummond, who was the first secretary general of the League of Nations, and Albert Thomas, who was the first director general of the International Labor Organization. These men held office simultaneously in the twenties and early thirties. Thomas was much the flamboyant active type and he got a good press, while Drummond was regarded as not very effective because he was quiet and anoynmous, the British civil servant type. And ever since people have talked about leadership in international organizations by reference to the Thomas or the Drummond model. Drummond was reported to have said, with some asperity and an obvious sense of jealousy about the attention that Thomas received, that Thomas could not have succeeded in Drummond's organization. He was probably quite right. The International Labor Organization and the League of Nations were two quite different organizations even though they were side by side in Geneva, and the style of leadership that worked in the one was quite possibly not appropriate to the other.

What if anything can we say in general about the essential qualities of leadership? Can we say anything at all useful that can be universalized in respect to past leadership? We have made some important distinctions; I think we should concentrate more on additional distinctions proposed during our discussions. Bailey's distinction between the mass and the entourage is quite a useful and fruitful distinction. There is obviously a difference between the task of getting support for the doing of a job from the masses and getting the job done by one's own staff. The doing of the job and the support from the outside for the job -- these are different functions. Leaders are in many respects foremen whose skill must lie not in doing things themselves but in persuading other people to do things the right way. There is a variety of power that entails actually doing a job. Another variety of power entails somehow managing other people, persuading others to do what one wants to get done. With my students I distinguish between the power of the foreman which is that of affecting the behavior of others, and what I like to call "Paul Bunyan power," with reference to that great mythical figure who was extraordinarily powerful but so far as I know never persuaded anybody to do anything. He simply went around cutting down the trees himself with one fell swoop of the axe. But by and large I think the function of the leader is to be the foreman rather than the Paul Bunyan, the axeman himself.

We find an additional distinction between gaining and holding a position and struggling for a place in the power pyramid on the one hand, and between doing the job for which the holder of the position is responsible, on the other. And there may be a conflict between these requirements. How to get the presidency and how to be the president and how to perform the tasks of a president, for example, are quite separable issues. And we are very likely to find that different qualities of leadership are required for getting and holding office and for running an office. To introduce another of my homely metaphors: I am impressed with the significance of what I call the Annie Oakley syndrome in the world of power. I refer in particular to the lovely song in Annie Get Your Gun, in which Annie says you cannot get a man with a gun. She was acutely conscious of the limited function of particular types of power. There are not many types of power that are all-purpose. Most of all leaders have to grasp what varieties of power are essential for particular tasks, and develop the necessary mixture of power capabilities.

Strong mentioned earlier the tendency of political scientists to concentrate on who gets power and stays in power, and to give less attention to what they do with power once they have it. We in the field of political science pay too little attention to public administration. We concentrate on making decisions and do not worry enough about implementation or putting these decisions into effect. A kind of happy Genesis conception of public administration prevails: God said "let there be light" and there was light, but it doesn't work that way in human affairs. You can say "let there be light" but then you have to make somebody produce light. You have to pay attention to the task of causing the desired result to come into being. That is where the effective leader has to know something about the nature of the power capabilities that are required for the specifics of his enterprise.

Well, I wonder whether the unlovely traits described by Mr. Bailey, the unpleasant behavior of the leader, his arrogance, his tendency to manipulate his staff, to divide and rule etc., are a part of the strategy related to the doing of the job or of the strategy related to the getting and keeping of the job. I suspect the latter rather than the former. These traits may be more pertinent to avoiding the usurpation of office by one's rivals than to getting the job of rulership accomplished. I suspect that most leaders will be concerned not so much with controlling the jealousies of their staff, but with getting the best work out of their staff, and different strategies may be in order. Indeed I am not quite sure whether in most cases these patterns of behavior are consciously adopted tactics, either for controlling the ambitions of one's underlings or for driving them into the performance of necessary tasks. Perhaps they are simply the inherent personality characteristics of the types of people who become leaders. Maybe leaders are by definition people who tend to behave in this way, not because they have a tactical notion about how to control their rivals or to manage their followers, but rather because that is the kind of people they are. We will leave that for discussion.

COHEN: Bailey's discussion of leadership and its entourage is, as he remarks, part of a larger study of leadership in relation to institutions and culture. And the study is certainly not meant to be prescriptive. Indeed, Bailey says that he cannot define what a leader is, and I am certainly not prepared to offer a definition. But in his discussion of the relationship between the leader and the entourage he draws attention to the uncertainty principle which takes place between the two. This strategy of uncertainty could involve the entourage as a threat or as help. Well this leads me to several questions: Does leadership involve virtue? Or are we to accept the fact that our description of leadership disregards its relation to virtue? If we disregard the relation to virtue, are we not in the descriptive mode committed to explaining why at one time leadership did involve a commitment to virtue? Are we not in the very descriptive terms of the paper required to explain how we got from a concept of a leader always committed to virtue to a leader who need in no way be committed to it? The eighteenth century is a kind of watershed in this respect. For example, Henry Fielding in <u>Jonathan Wild</u> has a long section on leadership. He says ironically that that there is no necessary relation between greatness and goodness. The traditional conjunction of greatness with goodness has ceased to be accepted.

The process of engaging in a description of behavior of entourage to leadership inevitably leads to a historical discussion of the relation of the leader to his entourage. If we characterize the leader-entourage model by the same principles as those governing FDR's relationship to his staff and cabinet, for example, are we not omitting those features which so distinguish this particular relationship as to subordinate the similarity of structure? After all, whatever we say about FDR, he did not shoot the members of his cabinet. Whatever procedures he was prepared to engage in to create an uncertainty principle, these were not the procedures of humiliating and then shooting them.

Bailey is persuasive when he draws attention to the fact that the closer the members of an institution are to their leader, the less they see him as a leader. In proverbial terms we would say no man is a hero to his butler. Now I find the implications of this very interesting in terms of our discussions thus far. It appears that those qualities that are identified with leadership -- and institutions as the mold in which leadership operates -- are necessarily connected with nonleadership qualities. Thus we need to recognize that a leader is imaged as a leader but, in actuality, recognized as one who is also not a leader. Now, in our society, where the visibility of leadership is available to all persons who watch TV, does this technology remove the distance and the image construction of a leader, or does this force the leader to become an actor? Does it force him into deceitful image-building precisely because what we did not have before, namely the capacity to view our leader under a great diversity of conditions, we now have: we can view him under these conditions which reveal his nonleaderly as well as his leadership characteristics. Are we at a time when nuclear leadership like the nuclear family is being replaced by multiple leaders, by leaders of interest groups? Are we now confronted with numbers of leaders? Does this mean that we are confronted with quite different, even opposed, leadership groups in the society and are involved in measuring one leader against the other? And are we developing a society where the notion of the single leader who speaks for all is no longer tenable?

One final comment. The papers before us and our exchanges draw attention to the rhetoric of leadership, a subject of great interest to Bailey. Now the rhetoric of leadership is not merely what leaders say, but what we who discuss leadership say about leaders. For example, the statements about Gandhi and Roosevelt are taken from books about Gandhi and Roosevelt, and Bailey's paper is thus an account of the accounts of others. This seems to me perfectly reasonable, but it means that our concern with the rhetoric of leadership may very well be a result of the breakdown of common guidelines about leadership. What we are trying to do, is to see if we can explain how the guidelines came to be broken, and rhetoric is of the clues. I shall read to you a statement made in Walter's book, Terror and Resistance, which is in Bailey's essay, to give you a sense of the way Walter is imposing himself through his rhetoric upon the reader. "The elders as in any traditional society not only served as the living archives of custom and law, but also exerted moral influence on the ruler." That is Walter talking. Not only do elders participate in important decisions, they also exercise restraint in various ways on the power of the ruler. Any innovating chief or king who seeks to rule without traditional limitations must deal with the resistance of the elders. This is Walter's view of how the elders were held in esteem before Shaka dealt with them. Walter goes on to say Shaka dealt with this resistance by redefining the status of the old men and then slaughtering them. When he says, "slaughtering them," he is clearly implying a certain immoral way of proceeding. Instead of respected persons who pass from active service to venerable authority, the elders were declared to be useless old women, unfit for fighting. It appears that before their extermination, Shaka had changed their status by instituted ridicule; he compelled them to wear petticoats of monkey skins shaped like the garments of old women for battle dress. All I want to draw to your attention is that the language in which Walter is talking about Shaka is more than mere descriptive language. Concealed in the description are a body of moral attitudes, a group of ideological assumptions, which as readers we are invited to share.

Is our concern with the rhetoric of leadership a result of what our discussions have pointed to, namely a result of the mixtures of certainty and uncertainty? Is our concern for the rhetoric of leadership and indeed for the concept of leadership the result of the decline of the notion of the single leader? Is the simple leader being replaced by consensus, by multiple leadership or by indirect leadership through the media? We must remember that our presidential leader, whether it is Carter or whether it is Reagan, assumes that the media has stolen from him the role of leader. These leaders claim that the media is changing the way people ought to think, not presenting the leader's views in a fair and purely descriptive manner. Finally in considering the rhetoric of leadership we must ask whether Bailey believes that holding a position of leadership endorses an individual with leadership qualities. After all, does the fact that someone is in a position identified or imagined as a position of leadership make him a leader? Is not one of the characteristic ways of referring to the presidency, to say that we should honor the office not the man?

BAILEY: Let me take the comments in order and see if I can undo one or two things that I see as misunderstandings. One concerns whether leadership is a matter of keeping the job or getting the job done, and Professor Claude came down in favor of keeping the job. Certainly leadership has to do with keeping the job, but I also think some of it at least has to do with getting the job done. Let me give some examples. Churchill provoked his followers to make them show their hands. Several sources indicate that Churchill did this deliberately. Roosevelt kept everyone on their toes and uncertain and unhappy as a way of keeping the followers in line. That sounds plausible to me and that is a matter of getting the job done. Again, there is an element of training in this strategy, as leaders have to face disappointments, failures, and uncertainties in the world; and thus to show the followers at home, so to speak, is a way of training them. But that is not the whole story. It is also part of keeping the job.

Claude also suggested that the leaders' methods are perhaps not consciously adopted strategies, but rather reflect the psychological quirks of the types of persons who become leaders. Indeed this may be the case but that is not my interest. Whatever leaders' motivations are, I do not know how we could ever get at them. I do not know whether a person could ever know fully or tell you truthfully what his or her motivations are. What I do know is how people interpret what leaders do. And thus in a sense I have put aside entirely the issue of motivation and have concentrated instead on the consequences or the effects. I am looking in other words at the culture, not at the person.

This response also applies to Cohen's comment on virtue. I will not attempt to say why leadership once involved virtue but now does not. All I will say is that I am not sure why he thinks that leadership no longer involves virtue. Certainly the image conveyed to the mass almost uniformly involves presentation of a person who is virtuous in the sense of brave, effective, and able to rise above the occasion and do what is necessary. It is only in the entourage that this picture is somewhat dented.

That leads me to a claim that Cohen suggests I might accept: No man is a hero to a valet. Well, I do not think I would say that necessarily. There is an element of overkill in my paper. The last thing I read before I came away was Alan Brooke's diaries. Brooke was chief of the Imperial General Staff, his book is about the years 1939-43. As chief of the Imperial General Staff, Brooke had the major job of keeping Churchill in order. Churchill had criteria about everything. He thought he was a kind of genius. He was all for action rather than thought. And Alan Brooke's job was to keep him there. There are innumerable wonderful passages in Brooke's book describing with considerable asperity how difficult Churchill was to work under. There are also passages from Brooke's private diaries, written for his wife and not, I gather, originally intended for publication. It is very clear in these passages that Brooke adored Churchill, and vice-versa. I have not developed this aspect in the paper.

The point I was making was that people in the entourage inevitably have a more realistic view. They do not necessarily see their leader as not a leader. Alan Brooke is very clear that there were wonderful leadership qualities in Churchill. He had no doubt about that. But he could also see what the weaknesses were. And whether you call this nonleadership or not, I do not know. I think Brooke would have called these weaknesses just plain, stupid follies that had nothing to do with leadership since they did not cause Churchill to neglect other aspects of the issue.

The contention that I am viewing leadership historically is a fair challenge to my essay. In order to see things in different cultural perspectives, I should see them historically, at different times, at different places, and so on. This is also a historian's point of view, but a comparative one. There is also a narrower meaning of history that studies the developmental process in the course of getting a following and establishing control. This process can be certainly pursued in terms of strategies and tactics that vary as time goes by and as the situation changes. I do not know quite how to respond to Cohen's question "Are we developing a society where the notion of the single leader who speaks for all is no longer tenable?" There is no single leader who speaks for all. I have never thought of the times changing that way at all. Certainly if there is an image presented in this country, it is of the leader. Now what the reality is like I am not sure, but I cannot see the kinds of qualities that we are talking about. The leader is one who can make a decision on no rational grounds whatsoever and yet convince other people that they should follow it. It is very hard for a committee to do that. Of course, they do it all the time but at least they parade reasons. On the other hand a good leader can do it.

As far as Cohen's point on the rhetoric of leadership, I think I am answering this imperfectly because I haven't fully grasped it. Inevitably, I do not see how I could have done anything else except take what people have written about leaders or leaders have said about themselves, because I was not there in Southern Africa at the time. The Walter book and those accounts before you in my paper were written at the time. The accounts give us a quite interesting basis for comparison, a glimpse in fact of two cultures. Granted, this "rhetoric" is riddled with judgements, slaughter and so on.

CAPLOW: I do not share Bailey's prejudices about leadership, though they are reasonable to have. It would be unfortunate if his pioneer discussion led to some wide acceptance of the rather negative view of leadership as primarily manipulative. Leadership is of course incidentally manipulated, but this can be done in various ways. Louis the XIV did not inspire the continuous terror that is so striking among the followers precisely because he had instead a fine definition of ranks, an elaborate protocol in which everybody's rank depended on his own. The royal officers did not derive their rank from the king and thus were not in that sense dependent upon him for the maintenance of their own position. They were dependent in another sense, however, because their positions were expressed in relation to his own. Louis' court was in continuous turmoil, all seventy-two years worth, over questions of protocol and etiquette which were unbelievable.

There was for example not one but at least fifty major episodes involving who might sit in an arm chair in whose presence. And many of them ended up before the parliament of Paris. Some of the cases dragged on for three or four years and involved hundreds of lawyers and a large expenditure, over the question of who might sit in an arm chair in whose presence. At one point an ambassador came from the newly installed King William in England to the Louis court; his sympathy turned entirely toward the new regime in England, who were considered as usurpers, because he had so perfectly mastered the French etiquette. In one case, after a long argument between subordinates he admitted that he need not greet the emissary from the top of the steps but said he would descend three steps and no further. And after prolonged negotiation that was agreed to.

Thus the whole elaborate system of etiquette was an interesting and complex substitute for terror. I believe Bailey oversimplifies a marvelously intricate and complicated subject. There are many devices for the maintenance of leadership. They do not, I think, primarily depend upon the realistic view of the entourage and the unrealistic view of the leader held by the masses, because the entourage may be very large and still appropriately subordinated by a leader who has the right kind of institutional devices. A leader who does not have a structure of protocol or a structure of traditional ritual or a system of competitive games or any other of the exercises that are necessary to validate leadership with an entourage, may very well resort to simple terror. But that, so to speak, is the most primitive operation of that kind in a society barely able to maintain any kind of large scale organization. It does not, I think, tell us that leadership is inherently terroristic.

Let me depart from Bailey's text a bit to elaborate on our earlier discussion of the crisis in the relationship between the citizen and the state. We discussed earlier the claim that the American presidency may be too much for any incumbent. It seems to me that in some respects our discussion may be moot. The problems that really ought to concern us may not be the problems of leadership at all, in the sense of the ability of the leader to measure up personally to the requirements of a position. But they may be much more about the absence of appropriate positions. The whole focus of modern leadership has been on the state and its dependent organizations. This has been less so in the West perhaps than in the East, but everywhere the state has grown to monstrous dimensions. Curiously enough, so far as I have been able to discover, not one of the fathers of modern social science, when he looked forward out of the 19th century into the 20th, had any glimmering of the forthcoming importance of the nation-state, and of the enormous vitality that nationalism would have for the 20th century. Quite the contrary. Most were persuaded, for example, that patriotism was a declining sentiment and would exercise negligible influence in the future. And Marx and Engels, and the whole line of Marxist thinkers, were quite persuaded that nationalism was only one of the numerous negative side effects of capitalism and would disappear peacefully as soon as the workers and various countries took power in their respective countries. Marx and anyone active in the development of socialist thought before 1920 would find the present relationships between the Soviet Union and China completely inscrutable.

So we have here the nation-state led very badly, and more particularly unable to cope with the principal requirements of modern society, that is, protection from technology, and the development of some kind of worldwide policy that can provide the minimum conditions of social order. And we have now a couple of generations later arrived at the point where we seem to be saying that social order is not possible given the existing structure of the world. If that is indeed the case then whether national leaders do their hopeless jobs well or indifferently well or rather badly matters much less than the fact that we have not yet evolved the kind of institutional structure within which the kind of leadership the world requires might occur.

SHANNON: Let me say that because I have no competence in my ability to speak ex tempore and because I have quite a bit to say I prepared my remarks which I will read. And let me say further that when I wrote these remarks, had I had the ideas that have occurred to me from these discussions and with Bailey's elaboration of his assumptions, his design of the whole study, I might not have written just what I did write. When I was asked to comment on Bailey's paper I agreed quickly because leadership of organizations of various kinds is one of my interests. My hope was that an anthropological study of leadership in a wide variety of cultures would reveal some similarities, some common aspects or features that, just possibly might reveal something innate in homo sapiens or, more probably, might reveal that human intelligence responds to similar situations in a similar way. When I read Bailey's chapter on leaders' entourages I was disappointed to learn that anthropologists have done little investigation of leadership.

Bailey's focus in this paper is the leader's entourage, which he defines as "subordinates who have a face-to-face relationship with the leader." He argues that "the principal strategy" that a leader uses "for controlling his entourage" is "not of trust and a sense of belonging (as in the case of a mass following), but rather the creation of uncertainty and discord and a feeling that it is even for himself. ...it pays the leader (up to a point) to keep the world of his immediate subordinates ... fragmented and at the fringe of their comprehension."

Let me examine Bailey's interpretation by seeing how it fits the facts, so far as we can learn the facts, of the entourage of President Franklin D. Roosevelt, perhaps with short forays into the entourages of other 20th century presidents.

In the abstract, logically, Bailey's argument is persuasive. It also fits roughly the facts how FDR handled his entourage. But I have some questions, some caveats, and perhaps suggestions.

An observation: nowhere in this provocative paper does Bailey say that a leader keeps the members of his entourage on tenterhooks as a studied, calculated, predetermined policy, but I infer, perhaps mistakenly, that he sees the strategy as deliberate. I do not think FDR's ways to manipulate and otherwise use his entourage resulted from a calculated decision; it seems probable that he arrived at his methods quite instinctively, although I cannot prove that.

Let me quote from Rex Tugwell's The Democratic Roosevelt (1957), a curious book in that it combines an insightful memoir with a conventional biography. Speaking of a disagreement with FDR about farm policy well before Roosevelt's first election, he made this intersting remark: "But I never won my point, in argiculture or anything else. Franklin took the advice which, as a politician, I suppose his instinct also approved. He left everything fluid, general, and discursive. He said as little as he could in controversial situations and left to the ministrations of time and his own mediating talents the issues thus remaining unresolved." FDR as president nearly always consulted and consulted and consulted with whomever he could in attempts to find as much of a consensus as possible. He consulted with leaders in whatever field was relevant -- agriculture, industry, banking, whatever -- with some of his aides in the White House, with some cabinet members, and with some senators or representatives. The few times he failed to consult widely and struck out on his own he hurt himself. The best example of failure was the Supreme Court issue in 1937. Before going to Congress with the Court proposal he had consulted only with Attorney General Homer S. Cummings.

The people in Roosevelt's entourage were quite heterogeneous in a variety of ways: in their personalities; in the length of time they were associated with FDR; in their backgrounds; in their party affiliations; in their ideologies, their ways of traying to understand the world and what they would do to improve it; in the nature of the positions they held; in the degree of their political support, their "clout."

How long and how well FDR had known the people in his "official family," as Tugwell called the entourage, apparently made a great difference. Louis McHenry Howe was easily the closest to FDR and had known him the longest, since early 1911 when as a newspaper reporter of the New York legislature he advised State Senator Roosevelt on political strategy. Soon thereafter Howe became FDR's professional political adviser. He became part of the Roosevelt family. Howe was FDR's secretary when he was Assistant Secretary of the Navy during the Wilson administration; he was with him in the 1920 vice presidential campaign and with him and the family when FDR was stricken with polio at Campobello. He moved into the White House with the Roosevelts and Mrs. Howe lived there too on her frequent trips to Washington. FDR and Howe made an odd couple. The patrician, charming, handsome Roosevelt was quite a contrast to Louis, who was without much charm and was a dirty, ugly, rumpled little man of less than 100 pounds who was chronically ill with respiratory and heart problems. Yet they were very close friends, and Howe was FDR's principal adviser on strictly political matters. It may be FDR would not have made his Supreme Court blunder if Howe had not died nine months earlier. At the other end of the scale were a few cabinet members FDR had not known long before he appointed them.

In between these extremes were the brain trusters, with FDR since March 1932: Sam Rosenman, Tugwell, and Raymond Moley. The ideological range in the brain trust was broader than one might expect. Rosenman was not very ideological; he was primarily an organizer, a head hunter, a ghost writer, and a superb editor. His editing of the several volumes of FDR's public papers and addresses was superb, and the set is indispensable. Tugwell, a highly intelligent professor of political science at Columbia who was so bloody handsome that his appearance probably was a disadvantage in dealing with men, was accurately known as a national planner, a planner in the sense that corporation executives are planners rather than in the way planning has been conducted in the Soviet Union since the rise of Stalin. Moley, a political scientist at Barnard when he joined the brain trust, was to the right of Tugwell. He broke with FDR later in the first term, partly because he thought he was launching a new career as a magazine publisher. All these brain trusters, incidentally, have written books about FDR which Bailey might find useful.

The cabinet members in the entourage, some of them only barely in it, were a special breed of entourage because, necessarily, they were chosen primarily for political reasons rather than for how they might fit into the group. And then there were senators and representatives from the Hill, who, it is true, did not meet personally with FDR as frequently as those who worked in the White House and, some of them, not as frequently as some cabinet members. Nevertheless, they met with FDR face-to-face more than occasionally, and they had many telephone conversations with him. These legislators constituted still another kind of entourage, a breed that came from both parties, represented a wide range of political views, and, most importantly, came closer to the degree of power that FDR held. Their cooperation was absolutely imperative if FDR was to succeed. Except in the first days of the first term in 1933 these legislative leaders were frequently balky, grudging, and obstreperous. In due time they would frustrate FDR time and again. The myth widely held by outsider conservatives, that Congress was FDR's "rubber stamp," is almost totally false.

Then, further down in the multi-decked club sandwich that is American government, were those who met with FDR only infrequently. Perhaps people at these levels did not meet Bailey's definition of an entourage member, but I have a little story about one such person that I cannot resist telling. It reveals something of FDR's personality and style. The story was told to me by Hugh S. Cumming -- not to be confused with Homer S. Cummigns -- who served as an executive assistant to Secretary of State Cordell Hull. Early one Saturday morning in September 1933 the 33 year old Cumming received a telephone call from a White House secretary. FDR wanted to see him in about twenty minutes to be briefed about the political and economic situation in Cuba. Having arisen only a short while before being summoned to the White House, the young man was frantic. He shaved quickly, dressed hurriedly, hurried to his office in the State Department to pick up some papers, and got to the appointment on time. When he was ushered into FDR's office the President did not even look up from signing some papers but told the young man he would be finished with the task in a few moments. Cumming stood quitely and apprehensively. Finally, FDR looked up and began laughing loudly. His first words were, "Mr. Cumming, I advise you that the next time you call on the President of the United States that you have your fly buttoned."

It seems to me worthwhile to read a perhaps overlong passage from Tugwell because it yields resonance to FDR's style with the entourage and its reaction to that style. It also tells us something about Tugwell.

> Franklin lunched at his desk, and never alone. Usually this was a time when one of his official family was invited, but seldom more than one. No one knew better than he the uses of consideration and even of prestige. The big men in Washington are very small about some things. They listen eagerly for gossip, especially if it involves themselves. They very quickly surround themselves with sycophants just as businessmen do, and usually they set up a spying organization to protect their empires from the inroads of rivals. They invariably have another organization to maintain their trading relations with congressmen, and they treat with the tenderest care their "information"

services -- those subordinates who maintain press contacts and strive to paint an approved picture of themselves for the public.

A President who knows his business watches these operations of his subordinates with tolerance and sometimes with amusement; he also makes use of it for his own purposes. He can do this very well because of his powerful central position. He can further or obstruct the ambitions of those about him without ever showing his intentions. He can smother their news, blur their picture, and worsen their relations. If they "get a little above themselves" he must do it, especially if their inflation threatens his own prestige in some way.

No President ever had a more intimate understanding than Franklin of these complex matters. He watched his subordinates at their games, checked them when necessary, contributed to their build-up when it was convenient, reprimanded them effectively by non-recognition, rewarded them by intimacies. Asking them to lunch occasionally was one of these rewards. Every other member of the official family knew that Harold Ickes, Henry Wallace, or Jesse Jones was lunching alone with the President; and everyone spent a little time considering what it meant for his interests. How this system worked under Franklin's management can best be understood by reading such a document as Ickes' Diary, those unhappy revelations of a perpetually sore heart. There was one period of more than a year when Ickes never saw his chief alone. On the other hand, very often Franklin had to tell him, or write a note and say, that he was indispensable. It depended on the circumstances.

Ickes was useful to Franklin in several ways, especially at first. He had been designated by the progressives, and they watched his progress with some vigilance. Later most of them were lost to Franklin anyway -- Hiram Johnson, Bronson Cutting, Bert Wheeler, Gerald Hye, Ned Costigan, and even Bob La Follette were all in one or another way alienated by the beginning of the second term; but by then Ickes had a reputation as an administrator which gave him some protection, and he had an unchallenged regard for the trust of his office which was not to be taken lightly, considering some of the unhappy experiences Presidents have had with Secretaries of the Interior. But he was a whiner, an egotist, and an incorrigible empire builder, He had to be kept in his place. But it had to be done without allowing his pique to overcome his ambitions so that he would quit. He was

92

always resigning and taking it back when reassured of Franklin's affection.

Some other members of his official family gave Franklin even more trouble. Henry Wallace, presiding over the agricultural sector, was a difficult inward-turning individual, but he had the best intelligence of anyone around and in a sense was the most loyal. He very early came down with the presidential virus, and this handicapped him in his office; but Franklin treated him very differently from Ickes, sensing his loyalty, his affection, and his genuine worth. He drew Wallace out, encouraged him, and until Wallace's services had been rewarded by the vice-presidency, never punished him as he was always punishing Ickes. His later annoyance with Wallace -- of which Jesse Jones was an equal recipient -- was an unusual outburst, a kind of exception, and shows how far Franklin's powers had declined in the later days of the war.

I have not much to say about the entourages of other presidents, partly because before FDR they were quite small and consisted mostly of cabinet members. Theodore Roosevelt worked very closely with William Howard Taft and Elihu Root. TR liked to refer to himself, Taft, and Root as the "three musketeers." TR liked Taft because he was amiable, able, and an excellent trouble-shooter. Woodrow Wilson, a gifted but strange man in many ways, relied heavily until 1919 on Colonel Edward M. House, who had no government position whatsoever. Other than cabinet members and congressmen, he seems not to have discussed policy seriously with many other people. Harding's entourage consisted of his cronies in Washington, many of whom were conspicuously corrupt. It is almost true to say Coolidge had neither friends nor entourage. Remember that he was an accidental president who never would have been nominated for the vice-presidency had it not been for the publicity he received during the Boston police strike and because the Harding ticket needed an easterner. Hoover, a hard worker who was admirably equipped for the presidency except for his incredible ignorance and innocence about politics -- the first public office he ever ran for was the presidency -- relied heavily on some of his cabinet members, especially Ray Wilbur, with whom he had been a student at Stanford in the 1890s, Arthur Hyde, and Andrew Mellon.

Before the great Depression, we should remember, entourages were small because government was small. The pace of government was slower, as was life in general. There were fewer major public laws in those early 20th century days, and most of them came from the initiative of Congress rather than the White House, as, indeed, did many passed while FDR was president. Nor did most presidents work hard or long. The frenetic Theodore Roosevelt was an exception of course, but he took a great deal of time taking boxing lessons, swimming in the Potomac, and what today we would call jogging. Before the war Woodrow Wilson normally worked only five or six hours a day, and he worked after dinner only in times of great crisis. When he worked, however, he was very fast and intense. Harding never worked very hard at anything in his life, except perhaps at chasing women, and Coolidge was well known for his afternoon naps, followed by long walks through downtown Washington accompanied only by a single Secret Service man.

Bailey has written a useful, intersting, and provocative paper. However, I remain unconvinced that an anthropological approach to leadership, or rather political leadership, provides a great deal of illumination on the subject. The differing structures and traditions of government and politics are vast, and they make an important difference in what a Zulu chieftain, a British prime minister, and an American president can do. We come down to this: successful political leaders are cunningly manipulative in most, perhaps all, cultures. And this is something that those who have thought much about it have known for a long time.

It seems to me that FDR's entourage and the ways he dealt with it were far more complicated than Bailey's construct permits, even though I think he is essentially correct. But Bailey redeems himself with a precautionary note in his prefatory remarks. He refers to a certain anthropological methodology "as a simplifying facade which makes the world appear less complicated than we know it to be: in other words, Ibsen's 'life's lie.'" That statement is true and therefore beautiful. Historians, of course, have the same problem. So do all people who seriously try to understand the world.

BAILEY: The respondent's replies have been very helpful and constructive. Several issues raised during our discussion require further treatment. One such issue concerns the expanding boundaries around and subcategories within the entourage. Churchill obviously had a whole set of rings of people around him, from close to very distant; he clearly (if he was smart) did not treat them all in the same way. Shannon raised a similar question: where do I draw the boundary between the mass and the entourage? I will address that question when I have to. A second issue concerns an expansion of leaders' activities. Yes, my paper certainly points in one direction -- toward the nasty activities, the manipulation.

A third question to be addressed concerns the leader's use of rewards to control his entourage. A good deal of exploration remains on different techniques and contexts which make one approach more appropriate than another. It is not solely a question of the personality of the person led, but also a question of what has to be done, how quickly it has to be done, at which time you can afford to reward the person, how important he or she is and so on. Rewarding is thus one way to keep the entourage in line that requires further exploration. The continuous consulting mentioned during discussion also merits further thought. The mediating talents referred to by many of the leaders discussed are a final issue for further study.

CAPLOW: Shannon has raised an interesting issue concerning the relationship between leadership and intelligence, reminding us of the activities of Louis XIV and Roosevelt, and of the relationship between a very capable man like Henry Wallace and FDR. Some of the people in Roosevelt's entourage were doubtless more intelligent than Roosevelt. Roosevelt did not after all have a massive intellect, or so we are told. I think there is not any question that Kissinger was much brighter than the Nixon he served. So what is the relationship here? It is obvious that in an entourage there are people who are highly intelligent. As professors we are often asked the question: "If you're so smart, why aren't you rich?" Well, the similar question could be asked: "If you're so smart, why aren't you a leader?" Why this strange lack of correlation between intelligence and leadership?

BAILEY: I do not think it pays leaders to be too clever. It certainly does not pay. A very clever man is also certainly in our culture the devious man: that is one point. The second point concerns the relation between the capacity to take action and the willingness to infinitely ask questions. I think this is the main consideration. A time comes when a leader says "We've talked enough -- we're going to do it whether you like it or not and whether I can justify it or not." That's not an intelligent thing to do, but it's very often necessary to do if you're a leader.

HARTT: I would like to see us address ourselves very briefly to a philosophic note to which I am profoundly committed, namely linguistic analysis, because we have several times mentioned throughout the conference, and now rather dramatically, several terms that are systematically ambiguous. And one of these is the one we have just been using, namely "intelligence." For some of us it clearly means what you call "quick study." For others it means creative intellect profoundly reflective. Clearly, in other context, by intelligence we really mean wisdom, the ability to discern a course of action proper to the circumstances. And to pursue it with intelligence, with proportionality, with prudence, etc. So when we pass out accolades to Jefferson as perhaps being the most intelligent I am not satisfied with that. I am not at all sure that when it comes to comprehension of the human condition that Jefferson is in the same league as Abraham Lincoln. But clearly we are using the terms "intelligence," "intellect," and so on, in different ways in that connection.

The second concept that simply cries out for analysis at this point is the concept of virtue. We are helped to an important degree in this point by saying that we have to distinguish

between one kind of virtue and another. The virtue of courage
for instance as distinguished from some other version, perhaps
the virtue of prudence. Old leaders, for example, may simulate
courage when in fact they are cowardly. That ought to tell us
something about the expectations of the constituency. That a
pretense of courage is viable. To pretend the power, I think
we would be hard put to think of an instance where that would
be regarded as some kind of a distinction between power and
virtue. Let us also come back to intelligence. Very few leaders
would simulate stupidity. They might pretend to have more
"intelligence," but they would rarely pretend to have less. Now
in terms of intellectual adornments, yes. We have had instances
in which the leader would pretend not to be superior in any
important respect to his constituency, but it would be a fairly
rare thing for a leader in any realm to create an image of stupidity. Now he might create the facade of stupidity, but want
to appear wiser than in fact he is.

That leads me simply to a third observation of something
that cries out for analysis at this point. It has to do again with
your notion of disposition. And that is the distinction that is
commonplace in philosophy, between motivations and intentions.
Now I think we are subscribing perhaps unwittingly here a great
deal to motivations. Not only in respect to leaders but otherwise. Regarding Bailey's claim on motivations, I cannot endorse
it as universal in its blanket form, as though no one knows the
motivations of another, perhaps not even his own. In respect to
one's own motivation, we may say that we stand on the edge of
mystification, but a normally reflective person knows the difference between the pursuit of self-regarding interests, whatever
those might be, and other regarded interests. So we have to
make a distinction between the mysteries of motives and the
normal state of our motives: namely our motives are often
mixed. Sometimes we do not know the difference between things
that are self-serving and things that are not.

One last observation on intentions. I think it would be a
very unusual thing for a ruler (not to say that it is not likely
to occur or that it never occurs) to conceal his intentions systematically. He may want systematically to conceal his motives.
But if he systematically conceals his intentions as the leader of
the state, then presumably he has betrayed his trust in his
people. So that to conceal his motives, that is to say in the
political realm of ambition, he does not have much of a chance at
that. Presumably he runs for office because he is ambitious.
But whether or not he is ambitious, he means to serve the
project, the end in view, etc. So as you pass from the anatomy
of motives to the anatomy of intentions, I think the function of
"deliberate deception" and so on itself undergoes important
reinterpretation.
BAILEY: I accept certainly what Hartt says about intentions.
One of the characteristics of leaders who are successful in

controlling their followers is that they have a very clear statement of what their goals are. And indeed if the goals are clear and are accepted by everyone, it is that much better. As far as the question of motivation, I think I want to stick to my enunciation. I do not think it is important to know what leaders' motivations really are. I think what is important is what interpretations can be made by themselves or by others about what their motivations are. We are not disregarding them. We are regarding them only when they come out of the psychic into the public domain. Then they are very important.

CAPLOW: This gives me a chance to introduce something that I could not for the world see how to introduce in response to Bailey. But it seems to me that the two questions you raised about the show of courage and the show of intelligence ought to lead us to think about something that oddly enough has not been mentioned. What I understand in the anthropological literature is called "dual kingship." This relates to the fact that in very many cultures chieftanship or kingship is distinct, and there are two persons, one who is a war chief or a warrior king and the other who is a high priest or mystical leader. We of course attempt, more or less, to combine those but not universally and probably the distinction always is maintained to some extent. The war chief has a simple intention to win his battles and in that sense he is a specialist in conflict whatever else he may do. And the high priest is one who, except indirectly, is concerned with the maintenance of virtue in the congregation. It seem to me that a great deal of intention boils down to those two things.

KHARE: At this point my concern is that the discussion has gone on in just one direction, that of micropolitics. Nobody has tried to link Bailey's concept of entourage to wider political issues or other institutions and their values. Except for Caplow, nobody has made an effort to relate the discussion to macropolitics. I will therefore make a comment in that direction. I shall amplify Bailey's notion of entourage in another direction, namely that of intrigues in entourage. Intrigues are part of the language of political struggle, and are variously reported from simple as well as complex political systems. They surround a powerful, autocratic leader. Let me give you an example from nineteenth century India, when in the north Mughal courts were declining and the British regents and Muslim Nawabs were jockeying for power. And among them different media were often employed to express such intrigues and to define, categorize, and classify different motivations and intentions. Just to give you an example, there was in the eighteenth century a ruler in India who was obliged to eat from six different kitchens every day. The kitchens represented major factions within the entourage of the Nawab. And to eat from those six kitchens in a certain sequence was to confirm his approval to those different factions. If he ignored one particular kitchen on one particular day that was a signal to the entourage that something was wrong or somebody from that segment of the entourages was becoming a problem. So the messages were being translated from culinary behavior to manipulation of the leader-follower interrelationships. Several such examples may be available of how intrigues form a regular part of the manipulation of leader-entourage relationships.

BAILEY: Both Khare and Caplow imply indirectly that the leader who does not manage his entourage properly is in danger of being politically emasculated. The function of the leader and the entourage is to deal with "the real world."

THOMPSON: Just two quick points. One, Caplow's last point comes fairly close to Cohen's point about virtue. One of the things that allows the consummate political leader to play these games, these terribly dangerous and unpredictable games, of dealing with his entourage, is that he seems to stand at any given time for something that is seen as being virtuous, something better than sheer manipulation. For at least some great statesmen these activities have been necessary concessions to the real world almost done in regret and remorse, perceived as falling short of something that is seen as better and more virtuous. Lincoln did certain things with anguish that one remembers in his behavior. The other point introduced by Caplow is the whole notion of the capacity for intelligence and temperment. When one recites the qualities of political leaders, in general it is not so helpful, it seems to me, to talk about abstract intelligence as it is about political intelligence. It is not so helpful to talk about morality as it is about practical morality, and the classics are full of discussions of this area.

I shall make one last point. Both the profoundest of the diplomatic historians and diplomatic analysts and the practitioners of diplomacy never for a moment thought that nationalism was dead. It was the men who erected edifices of thought like Marxist thinkers, like socialists, who talked about uniting. They imagined that this force was less powerful than it was. And one of the interesting things is the degree to which the great writers in diplomacy seem to understand this aspect with greater wisdom than do some of the abstract theorists.

LITTLE: Well, we have touched on the problem of virtue in leadership at various points and I am myself not fully clear on what Bailey's position on this particular subject is. It seems to me he fluctuates a bit from a fairly cynical definition of leadership to a desire to incorporate or at least tip the hat to the importance of virtues, dispositions, ideals and so forth in the assessment of leadership. The definition that I think you put before us is the only definition that we have had as such of leadership. Is this a correct reconstruction of the definition you put before us? A leader is a person who can persuade others to adopt a course of action as being rational or as being acceptable for which there is really no rational basis or no acceptable basis. I am assuming that is your view because it relates very clearly to your idea of a leader, that is to say the leader puts forward a set of essentially deceptive reasons for acting which have a persuasive effect upon his followers. However, they are deceptive because they have no basis in reality. Is that essentially your view of a leader?

BAILEY: I disagree with the word "deceptive," otherwise it is fairly correct. My position is that not all situations, but very many, are essentially non-computable. They are just too complicated to work out what the right solution is even if there is one. This state of affairs arises sometimes from sheer complexity. In other cases it arises because values, diametrically opposed values, are at play and there is no rational way of deciding between them. Both these situations mean that a decision is going to be made. And it is going to be justified in light of the belief (discussed earlier) that we are all going to be wiped out unless we do something about it. The leader means, "let's do something even if there are all kinds of rational objections that can be made." One objection is that such a practice involves deceit. It seems to me that deceit has the connotation of something wicked, something you should not do. I am saying that it is necessary.

LITTLE: Well, maybe it is necessary deceit or it is necessarily misleading, something of that sort. But you do mean to say that the successful leader is one who, perhaps with a benign intention, pulls the wool over the eyes of his followers -- to the degree that he leads them to think that he is doing something for a reason that he is not doing it for?

BAILEY: The sensible leader will, if it is at all possible, produce an apparatus of rationality to justify what he is going to do, whether it is the correct course of action or not. I do not even know if there is a correct one. Even if he cannot justify his decision he will say (and you must have heard this phrase in committees or somewhere else), "Oh well, we've talked for three hours on this, let's have a vote." And that is essentially a vote which is put before everyone there, and the decision is made like that. That is exactly like consulting an oracle or getting down on your knees and praying for guidance and so on, which is a nonrational but a necessary way of reaching a decision. That is what I mean by the quality of the leader. A person less than that is a manager. A leader is someone who can act, not only outside the established rules but also outside the rules of reasoning when he feels it is necessary, and can get away with it. If he does not get away with it he is not a successful leader. Further, a good reason can be given for saying we have talked enough, we have got to act. That seems to me not necessarily irrational in any case, but surely you want to preserve something like that as against the person who just by whim or caprice decides to do whatever he pleases to do. It seems to me those are very separable sorts of things; the one properly called irrational, the other not necessarily called irrational. For that reason Little's reconstruction of my definition, seems insufficiently sensitive to the complexities upon which decisions can be based and justified.

WOODARD: I would like to shift back to the issue of virtue that was discussed within a different context. We have been talking about the public leader essentially and it seemed to me the key there is the word "justice." "Justice" is the single virtue under which most leaders operate. We assume that a leader is there somehow to promote amongst the members of the society something that is higher than law, something that's higher than ordinary relationships are going to be, a just relationship. And it seems to me that historically the king, certainly in the Anglo-Saxon world, was always the reservoir, both the reservoir and the fountain of justice, a pure medieval metaphor perhaps, but the idea was that the king was somehow above law. Law somehow flowed from him. He had the responsibility in the old sense of "equity" of bringing to law that good judgment. At times it is a very wise king that can embody justice. This notion of justice, it seems to me, is important even with a separation of powers government. It reposes in the presidency a kind of pardoning power, a kind of judgmental power which is very essential to the notion of leadership, a power more than simply making decisions.

I would like to make just one further comment. Caplow and a number of others raised the issue about nation-state leadership: is it a possibility in the modern world? I think that if we look to the history of the modern state, it might very well not be. One reason the future of the state might not be very good is that the three dominant or dynamic forces in the twentieth century are all forces inherently beyond the power of the state. The first one is industrialism which is universal in character, and is becoming more so every day. We can see it stretching out in multi-national corporations and so forth. The second one is a kind of egalitarianism, conjoined with an international feeling of brotherhood, or a notion of international human rights. Both of these movements are beyond the control, or in some sense beyond the jurisdiction anyway, of any single state. The third force is that most potent power of science, which no single state can claim as its own, and which indeed stretches beyond the nation-state as we know it, literally insofar as the powers of reason prevail. All of this is to say that the state as we know it is a very new thing of course, as we all know. It is too small to deal with international forces that are really governing the modern world.

THOMPSON: Is not that part of the dilemma, though, that the state as we know it is obsolete and no longer adequate? But on the other hand, we have nothing for the political leader to put it in place. When I worked for a foundation that had an international program I did not have to pay a lot of attention for precisely the reasons you have mentioned. Many of the criteria of the nation-state science were universal and you could talk to a scientist in Nigeria just as well as a scientist in Columbia University. But for the political leader his awful dilemma is that he still comes to office to preserve the union. He still has the task of defending the nation and so you are caught in a situation where all of these insufficiencies are self-evident.

WOODARD: To reiterate, I think that the ideal element is one of just leadership. Anyone who is going to be a leader must be in some sense committed to the principle of justice. Now what you mean by justice and what I mean by justice and Adolf Hitler meant by justice are going to be totally different. But what they have in mind is an ideal component; it is that relationship that pulls people together within a sovereign state, and it can be worked out in a way that is more just than unjust. And it is through law or some other means that this will be done. I do not think anybody supports a leader who simply wants power. I think a leader must have some notion of how the arrangement can be put together ideally. He must be, as I said earlier, prepared to work within a just framework, or at least if he is not going to do that, maybe he would create a new structure or will step into the breach and create something totally new using his own personality.

BAILEY: I know that unless a leader's image is that of the person who can dispense a just solution, he or she is not a leader. And a footnote to Woodard's particular allusion to the kings and so on: When leaders propose from their position the ideal solution, they do not have to justify. Nobody says, "why did you do that?" And by virtue of the leader's position and charisma or whatever else it is, the leader has the right to say and nobody has the right to question. That is exactly what I meant by the word "reputation." Prudence is the word you were using.

WOODARD: I do not want to be heard to say that kings did not abuse power appallingly. But historically they always did it by use of a royal decree. They possessed the power to undo what the judges or the parliament did wrongly. For example, my job, my position as the crown, as the king, is that I have an over-riding commitment to justice to rectify abuses of the law, to make law better. So this language is always there. The abuse is there too undoubtedly. All I am saying I think is that the justification is linked to the idea of justice. I think that both are a part of leadership.

101

SESSION THREE*

APOCALYPSE: THE ULTIMATE CHALLENGE
TO LEADERSHIP
Julian N. Hartt

I

The tragic dimension of leadership is hardly to be treated seriously in so brief a compass. Yet not to treat it at all in a conference on leadership, given the historical situation, would surely be a more grievous fault -- even if none of us had grievously to answer for it. Accordingly, we are deeply grateful to Professor Roth for his discussion of a particular context in which the possibility of the Apocalypse is taken with the utmost seriousness.

It is fitting that Shakespeare should occur to us in this setting. And Sophocles, both in Oedipus Rex and Antigone. In our own national history the figure of Lincoln looms as the supreme symbol of the tragic leader; not only because he was martyred but, supremely, because he believed he was ordained, certainly by law and perhaps by Almighty God, to oversee a conflict more sanguinary, and in all more costly, than anyone then foresaw or desired.

I note, largely in passing, that Lincoln is an excellent test case for the clarity and fertility of Weber's distinction between

*EDITORS' NOTE: The following two papers are concerned with important humanistic issues in leadership studies. Since they stand by themselves and yet comment on what was discussed at the conference, they are included here essentially as they were presented.

the Ethics of Conviction and the Ethics of Responsibility. Lincoln's opposition to slavery has been rigorously examined in these late years by revisionist historians of various persuasions. Much is made of the fact that Lincoln accepted Seward's proposal not to issue the Emancipation Proclamation until a Union victory in the field was forthcoming. Antietam was at best a reasonable facsimile of that desideratum. The battle was fought on September 17; the Proclamation was issued on September 22. The transaction was clearly political. This does not mean that it lacked an ethical dimension or that the ethical was completely overshadowed. On his own recognizance Lincoln's first and overriding responsibility was to preserve the Union. Early and late he made it abundantly clear that in his view this nation was grounded in an ethical covenant. Its preservation, therefore, was at once a moral aspiration and a clear, if tragic, duty.

II

It was recently suggested in Science that among the faculties and departments of the contemporary university in America the Humanists are the likeliest to be pessimistic about the future. The author of this piece, Dr. Allen Bromley, distinguished physicist, found that social scientists are pretty much inclined to take the world as it comes "and not get excited about it." Natural scientists are the optimists. (Science, 26 Feb. 1982, Vol. 215, No. 4536, p. 1043)

Bromley confessed to "huge oversimplifications;" we are not likely to deny him that. I think something else is a more formidable shortcoming. That is the total omission, in an essay on "The Other Frontiers of Science," of any mention of the role of natural science in placing humanity on a new frontier: that dividing the kingdom of Life from the Kingdom -- so to speak -- of Death.

III

We hardly need to develop at length, or in living color, the nature of the Apocalypse thus prepared. We know that it has two components:

1) The destruction of civilization and culture as we know them; and

2) the extinction of the human species, the obliteration totaliter of a human future.

The first of these (1) is not problematic. Figures on the destructiveness of the nuclear arsenal are available. There are weapons in the stockpiles at least a thousand times more destructive than the bomb which destroyed Hiroshima and opened the Age of Apocalypse.

Given these realities, recent Administration proposals about Civil Defense -- mass evacuations and the like -- are the policy equivalent of a wholesale endorsement of Laetrile for the treatment of cancer.

On the other hand the second (2) component of Apocalypse, the obliteration of a human future, strikes us, initially, as implausible. Is it implausible on scientific grounds? Here we may be banking on ignorance; but not on the traditional ignorance of humanists relative to the "hard sciences." Ignorance, rather, concerning the proper extrapolation from the destruction of USA and USSR and western Europe to the destruction of human life on the planet. Perhaps the super powers are guilty of a peculiar form of hubris: their extinction means it is all over for humankind. Something of this sort was suggested, lopsidedly, years ago by Pravda in a review of the apocalyptical movie, On the Beach: the line was that it suffered grievously from Capitalist-imperialist weltschmerz. In a very different vein, though to a somewhat similar effect, in testing the waters of plausibility, the Washington Post recently quoted somebody in the defense establishment as saying that the loss of 500 million people in a nuclear war did not necessarily spell the end of humankind. Aren't we just dying to know what other details this sort of risk-benefit analysis might offer?

I suggest that the hard kernel of the implausibility of Apocalypse in the worst case (2) must be sought elsewhere. That is, in our conviction that rational people will not (would not?) permit the world to reach the point of No Return and No Future. Something like this conviction seems to be widely held, even though putatively rational people have nudged the world towards that precipice, that Last Frontier. Despite this history, most of us seem to feel that rational people in the critical positions of leadership would (will?) reach viable compromises, achieve effective resultions, before the Doomsday switch could be thrown. In the main we hold devoutly to this conviction, despite the fact that the conduct of relations between USA and USSR is much like a game of I Dare You. The realities reek with theatrical bluster and bluff and bullying. Whose turn is it to blink and back down? Who is keeping track, in a game in which the trump card is MAD, Mutually Assured Destruction?

IV

This pious, and arguably desparate, confidence in rationality in high places, is paradoxical, to say the least. The plight of intellectuals has its distinctive pathos here: we have drunk deep of the wells dug by Marx and Nietzsche and Freud; and thus have a rich potion of doubts about what goes on behind and beneath the facades of rationality. Yet the realities are such that we are constrained to believe that rationality in some element or form will reduce Apocalypse to the order of a nightmare diabolically intense in affectivity but insubstantial and ephemeral in actuality.

V

Here we have something wonderfully <u>theological</u>. Theological first in the contemporary pejorative sense: a tissue of counterfactuals and purely speculative propositions. Thereafter, theological in some richer sense. That is, we might just as well be deliberately and wittingly theological; and for a fleeting moment turn Platonic, indeed. <u>What kind of leader is called for by the threat of Apocalypse?</u> With what virtue ought he/she to be endowed? Virtues more than beneficient; virtues indeed salvific.

So let us begin where we left off, with <u>rational</u>. We forgot to ask what kind of rationality we were talking about, that has, in our terror-haunted imagination, salvific powers. For there are choices, after all.

(1) The rationality that is self-interest-calculative; best know laterally in its classical Capitalist formation, and in the historically correlative theory of national self-interest as the fundamental and perhaps overriding obligation of political leadership.

(2) The rationality that is the human-good-deliberative. Is this available and viable only in the "ethics of conviction," and not in the ethics of responsibility?

(3) The rationality of sweet reasonableness, comprised of prudence, and of a sense of proportion; and of readiness, as well as power, to control the passions, especially the negative passions -- fear, anger, hatred.

Proceed thence to courage, because decisions both unpopular and perilous have to be made.

Thence to sagacity, because unpopular and perilous policies have to be put across, they have to succeed, they have to win the people. What a challenge for the arts of persuasion! -- But we do not want, we cannot afford, sophists.

VI

Now for a swift return to the real world so-called. Are we asking for political leaders to be paradigms and paragons of moral sensitivity, who amidst all their stated and statutory duties, and with every self-serving interest in full display or waiting in the wings, will hold a watching-brief in behalf of humanity? Such expectations are likely to strike us as excessively unrealistic -- theological in the pejorative sense. But how else is the Apocalypse to be averted, put on the siding for another -- and we must hope -- interminable season?

As a people we do not consistently expect so much of our political leaders, despite the fact (though this may not be an exception) that a prominent component of the long-dominant civil theology was a conviction that in time of acute national crisis Providence has always provided the Savior-Leader. Otherwise expressed we do not consistently expect political figures to rise above the general level of moral aspiration and conduct. (In fact the Man on the Street is generally surprised to hear that a politician has attained the general level, for anything but image-purposes.) There are other kinds of leaders, leaders, that is, in other than the political realm. It remains a widespread, if no longer common, presumption that leaders on one realm particularly must be counted on to be effective, or at least articulate and persistent, representatives of the national conscience. That realm is Religion. I want finally to make some observations about the role of religious leaders relative to the Apocalypse.

VII

The picture here is uncommonly perplexing. A large component of the leadership of the main-line Christian churches in this country has regularly supported national policy, as defined by the executive branch of government, in times of grave crisis; perhaps never so evangelistically as in World War I, but nonetheless, predictably. Now a strong -- or at least clamorous -- rightist component, cross-denominational, offers unqualified support for the Reagan defense and international policies, and on religious grounds. In this view the ultimate earthly enemy is that incarnation, that apotheosis, of godless and amoral communism, the USSR. Preparation for the defeat of this enemy must be given the highest priority; he must be faced down wherever he appears, whether in Central America, or in satanically astute devices for keeping (Christian-Protestant) prayer out of our public-school classrooms.

I am not entirely sure whether the leaders of The Moral Majority are prepared to recommend all-out nuclear war in this their holy cause. In the 1980 elections their PAC correlates were remarkably successful in defeating McGovern, among others, preferring the charges that he was "soft on Communism." And there was Rev. Jerry Falwell's remarkable burst of NT interpretations: Jesus would have loved rockets.

On the other hand there is the rapidly growing, virtually explosive, movement, notably in the Roman Catholic leadership, demanding a freeze on the development or deployment of new nuclear weapons. It is far from clear whether this movement will make an effective political conjunction with the pacifist component long a significant minority in American religious left. (I do not mean to suggest that the Freeze movement has an overtly religious core, but only that religious leaders, Jewish and Christian, are visible presences in the movement.)

Those of us with long memories are now wondering about the impact of a conjunction of the Freeze movement with pacifist sentiment. Hitler was sure that the Baldwin government would not do anything to draw the fire of pacifist sentiment in England in 1936. Hitler's calculation was correct -- he brought off the remilitarization of the Rhineland without effective opposition. Thus another long step was taken towards WW II, to fall back on the wonderful wisdom of retroflection.

It is plausible to read some of the Reagan postures as warnings to USSR not to make a similar assumption about our will and our readiness to block further international aggression, even at the cost of enormous fiscal dislocations. But is this supposed to mean that we would embrace Apocalypse if only that would stop this enemy? Is it not the case that the improvement of our second-strike capability is designed to show the enemy that we can, an would, not only destroy his "will to resist" but his very existence?

I think we are entitled to wonder what seminal and controlling metaphors are imbedded in high policy today. One occurs to me; and need I say that in stating it I devoutly hope that it is not the dominant metaphor at work. Recall the last scene in Hemingway's For Whom the Bell Tolls. Robert Jordan, The American hero (?), injured badly, has been left behind by his company of Loyalist guerrilas fleeing from the Fascist enemy. Propped against the base of a tree, his submachines gun loaded and ready, he knows that he will die very soon. But he will take some of them with him, and thus insure the safety of his companions.

The metaphor has a long, long history. Thermopylae, three times the scene of heroic and losing battles. Arnhem in WW II. Custer's stand at Little Big Horn (no real hero, he!). And on and on.

The luster of the metaphor dims when it must compete with Apocalypse. Even Holocaust takes second place in competition with this theological-historical metaphor.

VIII

Jeremiah assailed the false prophets of his time. "'Peace peace! They cry, 'when there is no peace." (6:11) Perhaps what we need today is an obverse Jeremiah to say to the reigning powers:

Woe to those who think there is peace in the balance of terror. For they invest in the peace of all-inclusive death.

SHAKESPEARE'S IDEAS OF LEADERSHIP
IN CORIOLANUS
Robert Langbaum

Since this conference has been mainly concerned with modern ideas of leadership, ideas which mainly assume that democracy is the best form of government, it might be instructive for us to remind ourselves of traditional ideas of leadership, ideas which mainly show an antidemocratic bias. Shakespeare's history plays and tragedies are good sources of traditional ideas about politics and leadership, and of these his last tragedy Coriolanus (1607-09) is perhaps the best for our purpose for the following reasons.

The first reason is that Shakespeare's play is based on the Elizabethan translation by Sir Thomas North of Plutarch's The Lives of the Noble Grecians and Romans, which combines through North's interpretation of Plutarch classical, medieval and Renaissance ideas on politics, leadership and great men. Second, the play deals with a military hero who fails in politics. We often forget that heroism, success in war, was in premodern times the chief qualification for political leadership, as it still is in undeveloped countries. In Coriolanus, Shakespeare investigates the clash between military virtues, represented by the word "honor," and political virtues represented by the word "policy." Shakespeare is asking whether the hero can make a good governor, especially in a society like that of Republican Rome which contained a larger element of democracy than Shakespeare's own society. Third, as the great Shakespeare critic A. C. Bradley has noticed, Coriolanus differs from Shakespeare's other tragic heroes in that he lacks the imagination and articulated inner life which make them splendid poets. It seems to me that Shakespeare deliberately excluded imagination and poetry from Coriolanus (we get instead splendid rhetoric), because he did not want us to identify ourselves with the hero as we do with Hamlet, Lear and Othello; he wanted us to remain critical so we could judge the political issues.

The play opens with the common people rioting because there is a famine and they want wheat at a low price. They feel that the patricians are hoarding the wheat, and they particularly hate as "a very dog to the commonality" (I,i,29)[1] the military hero, Caius Marcius, later called Coriolanus to commemorate his conquest of the Volscian city Corioles. There enters Menenius Agrippa, an elderly patrician, who unlike his friend Caius Marcius knows how to use the politically appropriate language of moderation and humor, and is thus accounted to have "always loved the people" (I,i,53). In answer to their complaints, Menenius tells the people a fable about the rebellion of the body's members against the Belly. The moral is that the Belly stores the food so that it can distribute the food fairly to the other organs. I shall quote the fable, which comes from Plutarch, because it provides the traditional answer to the perennial question of politics -- whether rulers govern in the interest of themselves and their class or in the interest of society.

> <u>Menenius</u>. There was a time when all the body's members
> Rebelled against the Belly; thus accused it:
> That only like a gulf it did remain
> I' th' midst o' th' body, idle and unactive,
> Still cupboarding the viand, never bearing
> Like labor with the rest' where th' other instruments
> Did see and hear, devise, instruct, walk, feel,
> And, mutually participate, did minister
> Unto the appetite and affection common
> Of the whole body. The Belly answered--
> . . .
> . . . it tauntingly replied
> To th' discontented members, the mutinuous parts
> That envied his receipt (what he received); even so most fitly
> As you malign our senators for that
> They are not such as you.
>
> <u>First Citizen</u>. Your Belly's answer -- What?
> . . .
>
> <u>Menenius</u>. I will tell you;
> If you'll bestow a small (of what you have little)
> Patience awhile, you'st hear the Belly's answer.
>
> <u>First Citizen</u>. Y'are long about it.

<u>Menenius</u>. Note me this, good friend;
    Your most grave Belly was deliberate,
    Not rash like his accusers, and thus answered:
    "True is it, my incorporate friends," quoth he,
    "That I receive the general food at first,
    Which you do live upon; and fit it is,
    Because I am the storehouse and the shop (fac-
    tory)
    Of the whole body. But, if you do remember,
    I send it through the rivers of your blood,
    Even to the court, the heart, to th' seat o' th'
    brain;
    And, through the cranks and offices of man,
    The strongest nerves (tendons) and small inferior
    veins
    From me receive that natural competency
    Whereby they live; . . .
        . . .
    The senators of Rome are this good Belly,
    And you the mutinous members. For examine
    Their counsels and their cares, disgest (digest)
    things rightly
    Touching the weal o' the common (welfare of the
    people), you shall find
    No public benefit which you receive
    But it proceeds or comes from them to you,
    And no way from yourselves. What do you think,
    You, the great toe of this assembly? (I,i,97-156)

The parallel between the hierarchical organization of the body and of society is clearly antidemocratic. The fable of the Belly espouses the same conservative social philosophy as the famous speech in Shakespeare's <u>Troilus</u> <u>and</u> <u>Cressida</u> in which Ulysses explains that the Greeks are doing badly in the war against Troy because "The specialty of rule (the chain of command) hath been neglected," as has the "degree" (I,iii,78,83) or hierarchy which organizes nature and society. The problem is that the Rome of this play falls short of the conservative ideal. The patricians pursue their own interests, and the people consequently refuse to accept their authority. Yet the people, as they play shows, must be ruled one way or the other; for we see them manipulated by their own representatives, the tribunes. Despite the social disorder, a certain sociability and sense of community emerges from the good-humored exchange between Menenius and the people. This sense of community is quite broken when Caius Marcius enters, hurling insults at the assembled citizens.

<u>Marcius</u> . . . What's the matter, you dissentious
rogues

That rubbing the poor itch of your opinion,
Make yourselves scabs?

First Citizen. We have ever your good word.

Marcius. He that will give good words to thee will
flatter
Beneath abhorring. What would you have, you
curs,
That like nor peace nor war? . . .
. . . Who deserves greatness
Deserves your hate; and your affections are
A sick man's appetite, who desired most that
Which would increase his evil. He that depends
Upon your favors swims with fins or lead
And hews down oaks with rushes. Hang ye!
Trust ye?
With every minute you do change a mind,
And call him noble that was now your hate,
Him vile that was your garland. What's the
matter
That in these several places of the city
You cry against the noble Senate, who
(Under the gods) keep you in awe, which else
Would feed on one another? (I,i,164-89)

Caous Marcius is right, as the play shows, in saying that
the people require flattery as much as any monarch, that they
are fickle, ignorant, disorderly and self-destructive. Yet Shakespeare cannot conceivably expect us to approve of Caius Marcius'
rudeness; nor of his brutality when he says, in contrast to
Menenius' politic attempt to justify the authority of the Senate,
that he would like to subdue the populace with his sword.
Caius Marcius is not a conservative but a radical reactionary,
who would eliminate the plebians' traditional rights. The question for the critic is how Shakespeare has managed to justify
such an unattractive character sufficiently to make him a tragic
hero.

Caius Marcius' justification emerges in the war against the
Volscians, which he wins almost singlehandedly -- defeating the
Volscian hero, Aufidius, and taking the Volscian capital,
Corioles. His response to the extravagant praise heaped upon
him afterwards is admirably modest: "I have done/ As you
have done, that's what I can; induced/ As you have been, that's
for my country" (i,ix,15-17). He also refuses the larger share
of the booty offered him. His behavior on the battlefield is
exemplary; there his brutality in slaying the enemy is appropriate.

But Coriolanus, as he is now called to commemorate his
victory, cannot translate his military honors into political gain.

For though he is elected Consul by the Senate, he must also go into the marketplace in threadbare clothes of humility, show the people his wounds, and ask their approval of his election. This is cannot bring himself to do:

> Coriolanus. To brag unto them, "Thus I did, and
> thus!"
> Show them th' unaching scars which I should
> hide,
> As if I had received them for the hire,
> Of their breath only! (II,ii,148-51)

Democracy forces politicians into just such false positions. Coriolanus cannot compromise his motives or say what he does not feel. His justification is pronounced by one of two Officers who are setting up seats for the meeting of scenarios and tribunes which will decide upon the consulship. The First Officer says that Coriolanus "loves not the common people," but the Second Officer replies: "Faith, there hath been many great men that have flattered the people, who ne'er loved them; and there be many that they have loved, they know not wherefore (why)" (II,ii,6-10). What count are the man's deeds. His refusal to flatter goes with his refusal to hear himself praised. The scene turns decisively in his favor when he wittily explains why he will not stay to hear the Consul Cominius praise him in a speech which is one of the plays' rhetorical triumphs.

> Coriolanus. I had rather have one scratch my head i'
> th' sun
> When the alarum were struck than idly sit
> To hear my nothing monstered (made marvelous).
> (II,ii,76-78)

D. A. Traversi[2] thinks we are intended to judge adversely Cominius' description of Coriolanus' brutality in battle: "He was a thing of blood, whose every motion/ Was timed with dying cries" (II,ii,110-11). But since Cominius speaks only praise and since his speech is received as praise, it seems to me that we must accept the brutality as appropriate to battle and as adding to the scene's favorable turn toward Coriolanus. We are to understand that Coriolanus' noble sincerity is necessary to his heroism even if it unfits him for politics. The tribunes begin to turn against him at the end of the scene when, in lines 148-51 quoted above, he refuses to exhibit his wounds to the people as though he had got them for political advantage.

Coriolanus' absoluteness, the solitariness even of his military victories, unfits him, according to North's Plutarch, to be a "governor" because he lacked "the gravity and affability that is gotten with judgment of learning and reason." His is the uncivil "solitariness" of men "who will never yield to others' reason but to their own... For a man that will live in the world must needs have patience."[3] Coriolanus' tragic flaw, like Achilles', is wrathfulness. He loses his temper, says the offensive things that are on his mind, and so cannot gain political power. "His nature," says Menenius,

> is too noble for the world:
> He would not flatter Neptune for his trident,
> Or Jove for's power to thunder. His heart's his mouth:
> What his breast forges, that his tongue must vent. (III,i,254-57)

Coriolanus is too sincere, too noble for politics. Plutarch attributes Coriolanus' antisocial qualities to his lack of education; but Shakespeare links them inextricably to his heroism -- they are the price paid for his heroism. The heroic qualities are antisocial and antipolitical. That is why democracies are suspicious of great men as tending to be autocratic. Yet for a nineteenth-century hero-worshipper like Carlyle, who was reacting against the democratic preference for mediocrity, the test of a political system was its capacity to select great men or heroes as governors.

Coriolanus gets the approval of the people for his consulship. But their two tribunes or representatives, who want to destroy Coriolanus as a threat to the tribunes' power over the people, persuade the people to revoke their approval. Thus we see the people's fickelness and inability to think for themselves; they are always manipulated so that democracy is always a mere facade.

Coriolanus' mother, the only person to whom he is subservient, persuades him to stand trial to the people and to try with mild words to win them back. But at the trial he loses his temper, and the people upon prearranged signal call for his banishment. Coriolanus would have the patricians fight the plebians in his defence. But that is not the political way, and the patricians accede to his banishment to prevent civil war. In a subsequent scene, the tribunes point out to Menenius that Rome is peaceful since Coriolanus' banishment, and Menenius sadly agrees. The hero, so necessary in time of war, is a disruptive political force in time of peace.

The defection of the patricians, even of Menenius, shows by contrast the steadfastness of Coriolanus' fierce loyalty of his own idea of heroism. The self-justifying nature of Coriolanus' heroism becomes even clearer when he offers his services to the Volscian General Aufidius, his former mortal enemy, to fight against Rome. The two former enemies embrace and Aufidius assigns half his army to Coriolanus. In Aufidius' words, we see the self-justifying nature of heroism; for enemies can admire each other's heroic virtues with an almost sexual passion: "But that I see thee here,/ Thou noble thing, more dances my rapt heart/ Than I first my wedded mistress saw/ Bestride my threshold" (IV,v,119-22). We also see the self-justifying nature of heroism in the fact that Coriolanus behaves as honorably and heroically in fighting for the Volscians as in fighting for the Romans. The purpose does not matter so much as the professional <u>virtu</u>. The ethic involved is heroism for heroism's sake; just as three and a half centuries later we begin to hear about art for art's sake.

Together Aufidius and Coriolanus swiftly conquer Roman territory and are soon at the gates of Rome. A. C. Bradley points out that Shakespeare's Coriolanus plans a revenge not in Plutarch -- he plans to burn down Rome. Coriolanus' "blind intolerable chaos of resentment," says Bradley, "conceives and gives birth to a vision, not merely of battle and indiscriminate slaughter, but of the whole city one tower of flame ... What controls him is the vision that never leaves him and never changes, and his eye is red with its glare when he sits in his state before the doomed city."[4] This vision, which externalizes the raging fire within him, signals the mightiness of his wrath. The vision is self-destructive; for he does not stop to consider that in burning Rome, he will burn up his mother, wife and son. Nor does he consider -- as the audience, I think, faintly does -- that there remains in him a core of humanity which will not let him carry out so drastic an enterprise. The raging fire within him combines with his human hesitation to externalize the fire to give him tragic stature and bring on his tragic end.

His tragic end is also brought on by the extraordinry prowess in battle which makes him a hero among the Volscians and thus awakens Aufidius' jealousy. Awaiting the opportune moment, Aufidius has Coriolanus assassinated in the end before he can prove his innocence to the Volscians, who accuse him of treachery when he retreats from the common purpose of conquering Rome. Once again Coriolanus is defeated by intrigue. A master of overt aggression, he is helpless before hidden aggression. Coriolanus' character is defined and justified by comparison to Menenius, on the one hand, who is genial, rational and politically adept but definitely not a hero, and by comparison, on the other hand, to Aufidius who is heroic but less heroic than Coriolanus. One cannot conceive Coriolanus feeling jealous or participating in intrigue. His flaws stem from his sincerity and outspokenness.

Aufidius, in the scene where he decides to destroy Coriolanus after he has served the Volscians' purpose, realizes Coriolanus' superiority to himself. Coriolanus, he says, will be destroyed by his very virtues and his very success: "He has a merit/ To choke it in the utt'rance" -- "a merit," as the editor explains, "that is nullified in the very act of being expressed because of faults inseparable from the particular virtues being praised."

So our virtues
Lie in th' interpretation of the time;
And power, unto to itself most commendable,
Hath not a tomb so evident as a chair
T' extol what it hath done.

The "chair" is that of the speaker who praises the virtues that led to power. So, Aufidius concludes, one virtue destroys another and a great man is brought down by his success: "one fire drives out one fire; one nail, one nail;/ Rights by rights founder, strengths by strengths do fail" (IV,vii,48-55). With Coriolanus and the Volscians at their gates, the Romans turn to mutual accusation. Menenius accuses the tribunes of stirring up the people against Coriolanus, but admits that the nobles were "cowardly" (IV,vi,123) to give into the mob. The plebians now deny that they wanted Coriolanus banished: "I ever said we were i' th' wrong when we banished him" (IV,vi,155-56). They have arrested one of their tribunes and threaten to execute him if Coriolanus does not relent. Plebians and patricians sway with the winds of change for their own advantage. Only Coriolanus remains steadfast. When he relents, it is because he has discovered at a deeper level of his nature a principle more fundamental than revenge. The change of mind is his glory but leads to his downfall.

Emissaries are sent to Coriolanus to beg for mercy. All in vain. He even rejects the plea of his spiritual father Menenius, telling Menenius that he has renounced all ties with Rome: "Wife, mother, child, I know not" (V,ii,83). This, as the audience suspects, is too extravagant a statement; Coriolanus thinks himself more hardhearted than he is. It is a fine Shakespearean touch that just before his wife, mother and child enter, he renews to Aufidius his vow to reject all pleas from Rome, then wonders on hearing the sound of new arrivals, whether he will have the strength to maintain his resolve so much has the rejection of Menenius strained him: "Shall I be tempted to infringe my vow/ In the same time 'tis made? I will not" (V,iii,20-21).

Although wife, son, and a fiercely patriotic Roman virgin are present, the ensuing scene is played out between Coriolanus and his mother. The scene turns on Coriolanus' violation of the natural order in renouncing country and family. "But out, affection!" he says on seeing his family enter,

All bond and privilege of nature, break!
... I'll never
Be such a gosling (as) to obey (family) instince, but stand
As if a man were author of himself
And knew no other kin. (V,iii,24-37)

There is in this a <u>hubris</u>, a sin of pride, which calls for retribution. To compound his pride and make his reversal even more spectacular, Coriolanus asks Aufidius and other Volsces to remain present as witnesses to his steadfastness.

Coriolanus' violation of nature is brought home to him when he kneels to his mother but she insists that he stand up while she kneels to him instead.

> <u>Volumnia</u>.   O, stand up blest!
> Whilst with no softer cushion than the flint
> I   kneel   before   thee,   and   unproperly   (for   a
> mother)
> Show duty, as mistaken all this while
> Between the child and parent.

"What's this?" exclaims Coriolanus. "Your knees to me? To your corrected son (corrected by your kneeling)?" Then all nature falls into disorder: "Then let the pebbles on the hungry beach/ Fillip (strike) the stars! Then let the mutinous winds/ Strike the proud cedars 'gainst the fiery sun" (V,iii,52-60).

Volumnia shows that Coriolanus has created both personal and public disorder.

> <u>Volumnia</u>.   thy sight, which should
> Make our eyes flow with joy, hearts dance with
> comforts,
> Constrains them weep and shake with fear and
> sorrow,
> Making the mother, wife, and child, to see
> The son, husband, and the father, tearing
> His country's bowels out.

It is a sign of our unnatural situation that our loyalties are now divided:

> Alas, how can we for our country pray
> Whereto we are bound, together with thy victory,
> Whereto we are our bound?

The victory of one means the defeat of the other. So intertwined are the public and private realms -- the intertwining distinguishes traditional from modern political theory -- that in marching "to assault thy country," you will "tread/ ... on thy mother's womb" (V,iii,98-124). The play's single-minded concentration on divided loyalties, to the exclusion of the usual Shakespearean subplots and comic relief, combines with the consistently high rhetoric to make <u>Coriolanus</u> the tragedy of Shakespeare's which more resembles the tragedies of Corneille and Racine. That is why <u>Coriolanus</u> seems "cold" to tastes schooled in Shakespeare's other plays.

Coriolanus remains adamant. Two items in Volumina's final speech, however, change his mind. The first is her statement that she does not want him to betray the Volscians but to reconcile them with the Romans. The other is her parting gibe as she prepares to leave in defeat.

> <u>Volumnia</u>.   Come, let us go.
> This fellow had a Volscian to his mother;
> His wife is in Corioles, and his child
> Like him by chance.

Such ironic intertwining of his political and familial defection makes Coriolanus realize that he has violated not only the natural and social order but the deepest stratum of his own nature. He holds his mother's hand silently.

> <u>Coriolanus</u>.   O mother, mother!
> What have you done? Behold, the heavens do ope,
> The gods look down, and this unnatural scene
> Thay laugh at. O my mother, mother! O!
> You have won a happy victory to Rome;
> But, for your son -- believe it, O, believe it! --
> Most dangerously you have with him prevailed,
> If not most mortal (with deadly results) to him.
>   (V,iii,177-89)

The whole tragedy is condensed in the pathos of this speech. Through my capitulation, Coriolanus is saying, order will be restored ("the heavens do ope,/ The gods look down") -- but at the price of my death. He is seeing through, not only to his own death which will follow swiftly, but to the deep structure of all tragedies: order is always restored through the tragic hero's death. He is also seeing through Volumnia to the archetype of the Great Mother as creator and destroyer.[5] Once before Volumnia has given him destructive advice, when she persuaded him to permit the trial which led to his banishment. Yet she is right, and he is right to capitulate. For he is discovering and bringing to fruition his humanity.

Immediately after this scene, we return to Rome where Menenius, who has not yet heard the news of Coriolanus' capitulation, assures one of the tribunes that Volumnia will not prevail because Coriolanus is not human: he is like an engine, a statue, a god. "There is no more mercy in him than there is milk in a male tiger" (V,iv,19-30). This speech, in which Menenius knows less than we do, helps us measure the amount of Coriolanus' improvement. A few lines later Menenius receives the news of Coriolanus' capitulation to his mother.

Modern readers cannot be sure how to take this strong man's devotion to his mother. Is it the chink in his armor, or is it a virtue? For post-Freudians such devotion is suspect as Oedipal. But for premodern readers, it was probably a sign of proper filial respect; and in the case of an enginelike, godlike hero (Achilles was also devoted to his mother) a sign of his humanity. It is difficult to know whether Shakespeare is psychologizing the situation and wants us to understand that heroes are overgrown boys. Such an analysis would account for Coriolanus' inability to be political. It is borne out by the fact that Aufidius, when he accuses Coriolanus of treachery before the Volscians, calls him "thou boy of tears!" Coriolanus is so stung by this insult that he repeats it three times, losing his temper and reminding the Volscians, in a most impolitic way, how many of them this "boy" did away with. "'Boy!'! O Slave," he says.

> Coriolanus.   "Boy!" False hound!
> If you have writ your annals true, 'tis there,
> That, like an eagle in a dovecote, I
> Fluttered your Volscians in Corioles.
> Alone I did it. "Boy?" (V,vi,101-117)

In losing his temper and playing so easily into Aufidius' hands, Coriolanus shows that he is indeed a boy.

Reminded of the relatives Coriolanus has killed, the enraged Volscian people call for his death and the conspirators, on signal from Aufidius, kill him. We are not to take it as ironic that almost immediately afterward Aufidius pronounces the final speech of praise which concludes all Shakespeare's tragedies.

> Aufidius.   My rage is gone,
> And I am struck with sorrow. Take him up.
> Help, three o' th' chiefest soldiers; I'll be one.
> Beat thou the drum, that it speak mournfully;
> Trail your steel pikes. Though in this city he
> Hath widowed and unchilded many a one,
> Which to this hour bewail the injury,
> Yet he shall have a noble memory. (V,vi,
> 147-54)

Partly Aufidius is in this speech the spokesman for Shakespeare, who is telling us that the dean man is a tragic hero, too noble to have succeeded in this world but fulfilled through his death both as a hero and a human being. Shakespeare is also showing us through Aufidius that order has now been restored so that even the dead man's enemy can now afford to praise him. Partly also, however, Aufidius is speaking in character as a hero who is paying tribute to the self-justifying heroic qualities in his enemy and recognizing, as he always did, Coriolanus' superiority to himself in those self-justifying heroic qualities.

What then is the play's political point, what are the play's ideas about leadership? The play is telling us that heroes are necessary in war and that afterward the best thing to do with them is to give them a splendid tomb and lots of praise. They are misfits in the body politic, because heroism is a lonely enterprise based on high principles that cannot be compromised. Heroism therefore cannot be reconciled with the daily trivial business of society and with the complexity of conflicting interests. The hero stirs up rather than helps to settle disagreements. We see how, even at the last minute before his death, Coriolanus throws the Volscians into a rage. Yet society needs heroes and the memory of heroes as a model toward which to strive, even though society will never arrives at nor want completely to arrive at the condition proposed by that model.

NOTES

[1]Quotations will be from the Signet edition of William Shakespeare, The Tragedy of Coriolanus, ed. Reuben Brower (New York and Toronto: New American Library; London: New English Library, 1966).

[2]D. A. Traversi, An Approach To Shakespeare (London: Sands, 1938). The chapter on Coriolanus is reprinted in the Signet Coriolanus.

[3]Plutarch, The Lives of the Noble Grecians and Romans, tr. Sir Thomas North, ed. W. W. Skeat in Shakespeare's Plutarch (1895). The chapter on Coriolanus is reprinted in the Signet Coriolanus, quotation from p. 223.

[4]A. C. Bradley, A Miscellany (London: Macmillan, 1929). Bradley's lecture on Coriolanus is reprinted in the Signet Coriolanus, quotation from p. 261.

[5]See Erich Neumann, The Great Mother: An Analysis of the Archetype, tr. Ralph Manheim (New York: Pantheon, 1955).

SESSION FOUR

CONCLUDING REMARKS

KHARE: This is the last session of this conference. I shall perform my duty as an organizer by identifying three general points that could be taken up for further consideration. First, the participants may draw attention to those aspects of leadership that are relevant to our concerns but have been overlooked. Second, this is the time to develop summaries, overviews and perspectives on both micro and macro aspects of leadership. Third, the participants are invited to offer their comments on leadership as a topic for further research and exploration. The last may be particularly appropriate for a committee such as ours.

I may remark in general about certain points already discussed in the conference. We have drawn heavily upon a discussion of political strategies and their significance for leadership. Bailey's micro-level discussion of entourage focused our attention on this problem, but only to raise the much larger issues of values, intentions, motivations, and meanings which leaders draw upon to remain in power to implement what an optimist would term the "public good." Whether a skeptical mind finds leaders to be manipulators only raises a provocative point, but it does not alter the social fact that various societies keep relying on leaders for practical as well as ideal reasons.

ROTH: I would like to try to summarize my perceptions, beginning with the most abstract statements and working my way to some contemporary political issues. From there I will propose some topics that might be explored along the major interests of the group in leadership.

125

Let me begin with a few remarks on the difference between a micro approach and a macro approach. Despite the prevailing structurism current in social science, I find the need to emphasize or re-emphasize a historical approach. I enjoyed very greatly Professor Bailey's micro analysis of leadership, in part because I too have tried to show universal elements of what I prefer to call personal rulership through the ages, through the third-world, and through highly industrialized countries. It is a most legitimate way of looking at more or less permanent features. However, our discussion will not be furthered if I now simply adopt Bailey's tough-minded characterization of leaders. I would like to emphasize instead the burdens of leadership, especially in a highly complex modern society. I remind you of a term which I think goes back to Benjamin Nelson, the sociological reality principle, and of what was for Nelson a Weberian position, namely the inescapable need for large scale organization in a highly complex society. Somebody must be willing to carry the burdens of leadership. Now Bailey's position may be that there has been too much glorification of leadership, beginning with the glorification of kings and warriors. My answer would be that from anthropology to history there is in a way too much structuralism. Problems of leadership are easily pushed aside nowadays in the name of the great waves of historical development.

My own concern is directed against the present tendency, ranging from anthropology to sociology and even history, to do away with the history of events and with political history, and therefore also to ignore the problem of leadership. And while it is course true that the high and mighty in the world have had their legitimate grievances throughout the ages, I would charge many of my colleagues in the social sciences with a profound anti-institutional bias, against which I would like to uphold the sociological reality principle.

Let me move from these general remarks to remind you that my specific purpose here has been to divert attention from problems of charismatic leadership to Weber's general sociology, by which I mean his notion of developmental history. I have demonstrated the connection between Weber's generation of economic historians and what then turned into the French structural history. And here I may respond quickly once more to Woodward: if we study the uniqueness of the West in terms of the developmental perspective extending over two and a half thousand years, we discover a distinctive notion of Western rationalism that alone does not tell us what we should do in a political crisis. What we acquire from Weber is an ambivalence towards this Western rationalism, towards its unique achievements and its corresponding profound dnagers (for us and for the rest of the world).

Moving to the political level, I suggest that insofar as the ethic of responsibility is not an abstract scheme of reflexivity, it

126

is necessary to give it a somewhat different, if not decisively different, concrete content. I suspect, as you remember from my paper, that behind Weber's notion of the ethic of responsibility was indeed an older classic notion of the balance of power. This notion simply must be revised under the current circumstances. I did not include in my paper a speech Chancellor Schmidt gave recently in West Germany, where he claimed that peace should be considered a basic human right, a claim underscored by the need for continuing disarmament efforts. My most specific political argument would be that the fate of the world must not depend on whether or not the Soviet Union and the United States are willing to sit together. They must be pushed to sit together. Europe must play a rather active role, and somebody must be the interlocutor or interpreter in terms that have recently been used to describe Schmidt's effort: Everybody tries to stay clear of the role of the honest broker, a role ascribed to Bismarck when he attempted to negotiate an international settlement between Russia and Western countries.

Let me now note briefly at least one possible direction in which our concern with leadership could be pursued. I think it is quite legitimate that some of you want to be faithful to the older traditions and to reflect on what constitutes great leadership. In a more empirical vein, one interesting phenomenon to pursue is the fact that in some Western countries the peace movement does not have a centralized leadership. It is simply not true that the collection of one million signatures in West Germany was due to some communist conspiracy, that funds were funneled from the East and that communist groups then manipulated a national organization. It was a vast grass roots effort in which of course some extreme left wing groups were involved. But there were many, many other people. The striking thing about the peace movement in Western Europe (and it seems to follow a similar course in the United States) is that there is no central organization, that it does not depend on charismatic leaders to emerge, and that indeed it is a vast or at least a large grass roots movement. In fact it may have so many centrifugal tendencies that it will not ultimately be able to impinge on the national leadership.

A parallel phenomenon is that party structures remain intact in Europe in contrast to the United States, where one finds no functioning parties and therefore also no national leadership in the European sense. One cannot groom people, members of parliament, to take over leadership in ten and twenty years. This country is in a desperate situation in that one never knows where the next President will come from, and then after four years, if he is unlucky, he will disappear never to be heard of again. It is a very dubious way of running the biggest country in the world in my judgement.

Let me make the last point. What is happening in Europe, despite the existing party structures, is a fragmentation within the parties from right to left. So that, parallel to the grass roots movement of the peace movement, there is a grass roots movement in the parties which makes it harder and harder for national leadership to arrive at compromises which can be sustained in the foreseeable future. This problem is sometimes described as the ungovernability of Western democracies. Certainly in Western Europe, in small countries as well as large countries, we have now a very delicate situation. Some countries seem to approach the Italian situation, where governments rise and fall, and as long as they are in power there are very precarious compromises that cannot provide any viable political leadership.

BAILEY: There are two issues that you might think about when this symposium is put together. I shall argue that micro studies are an essential underpinning of macro studies. When we do not understand what is going on, we come too quickly to a prescription before we know what we are prescribing about. "Micro" has the unfortunate connotation of being small and therefore unimportant. The micro world that I am talking about is the world of leaders and statesmen who do make decisions, and who do have an influence on the world. And at micro level, when we are addressing the politics of debate between persons, face to face antagonisms and so on, it is inevitable that the institutional framework should somewhat recede. If we stand far enough back, the institutions stand out as important and the individual leaders themselves appear small. When we sit close in the room with them, the leaders become big and the institutions become little.

Now, what is it that we are studying? Well, I know, or I think I know, what I am doing with my life. I want to understand what people think and feel and why they think and feel that way. When I have done that I may feel like telling other people how to run their world. But until I have done that I do not want to. So what is it that we are studying? Well, I have been pressed throughout to say what is an ideal leader and a good leader and so on. And I have resisted throughout, not because I do not think I do not know, but rather because I do not think I know in any scientific way unless one tells me about the circumstances. At one level there is an ideal of the leader, and a lot of our discussion has referred to this ideal. And then at the other level there are the actual leaders who do less than the proper things that a good leader does. For example, Kenneth Thompson gave us an admirable list of qualities and performances that we expect from an ideal leader. And when we look at actual leaders we can see the deficiencies.

If we look at the culture of leadership we somehow overcome these problems. We are still away from the real world. But at least within a culture there is combined both people's ideas of what the good leader is and people's expectations of what leaders will actually do. Now that is still one step removed from what actually happens. But I think that is probably as near as we can (or as near as I want to) try and get. This is not the ideal. I am not saying what the good leader is. I am saying instead what in culture x or society x is considered to be a good leader and what in country x or society x the actual leaders are expected to do.

Let me return to the point I made at the beginning: this kind of knowledge is absolutely necessary if one has any interest in social engineering, which in fact is what the macro half of the conference is talking about. Unless we know how people see their world (as it is and as they would like it to be), we are not able to make sensible prescriptions for what should be done to bring about whatever goals deemed proper. A related point concerns the study of leadership, and the question "are leaders important?" Well, there is of course the well known debate. The leaders themselves certainly think they are important. My paper contains many quotations where leaders make it quite clear that the world would be a different place if they had not been in it and had not done what they did. And then there is another school which says that leaders are merely spawned by circumstances, it does not really matter who they are. The leaders imagine that they are steering the ship but in fact the current and the winds are so strong that they go where those currents and winds go. They have no importance in shaping the world. They are necessary certainly, but they are merely necessary as facilitators for the continuance of these currents and winds.

I think this debate in the end is not worth pursuing, except in the following respect. I think there is an esthetic pleasure in puncturing some of the pretensions of leadership. I have been reading so many biographies; I know there are people like Montgomery who is wonderfully self important, but it is very nice to think that even people of that ilk are healthier after deflation. And there is a more serious side to this. Do not forget that the ideal leader dispenses justice. But the actual leaders often did not dispense justice, and the business of ridiculing them, of making them smaller than they think they are, is one way of controlling them and is therefore to my mind important. If there is an objective truth in this particular debate it is clearly that the truth lies somewhere in between. Of course leaders are constrained like everybody else by the forces around them. However, leaders are people who are capable of taking initiative, who have a superior capacity for taking initiative, who can act when they cannot show the reason for acting, but who have the courage to do so. It is necessary in the study of leadership to understand the cognitive and affective matter, not only of the leaders but also of the people who are led, and still more importantly, of the people who resist leadership and refuse to be led.

COHEN: As one who is not a student of the field of leadership, what I shall try to do is to present what I have learned from the different speakers and to lay out what I think has been offered at the conference. And I do this by dividing my responses into four areas. I begin with trying to locate the subject matter of leadership that we have been discussing. I believe that our subject matter has been primarily a study of the holders of political power and their followers. But mention was also made of the holders of military or religious power and their followers. And incidentally, offered for consideration but not discussed, was the function of those who exert modeling or shaping behavior as artists or teachers on followers or on groups of followers. This seemed to constitute the subject matter of leadership and those who can be considered leaders.

The second subject that was covered had to do with a study of the exercise of leadership. I think that our study involved three areas. One was the individual leader. The second was the institution of which the leader was a part. And the third was the culture in which this institution was to be found. We found that the individual leader could be understood as possessing some transactional relationship with his followers, identified in Bailey's terms as "entourage" or "staff." And that this transactional relationship involved threat and thanks, carrot and stick, reward and punishment. The individual leader has at different times different ideal qualities appropriate to the situation of leadership. The defeat of a leader could be attributed either to competition from competing leaders or to his own combination of leaderly and unleaderly qualities in which the unleaderly become dominant. With regard to the institution, the argument was made that the institution legitimizes power and authority and that the leader could either advance the institution or hide behind it so that we need to distinguish between the authority of the position and the role of the leader. Now these can be seen as distinctions although sometimes obviously united. With regard to culture, I believe we made the following points: that the culture serves as a kind of system which perpetuates or permits ideas of leadership. Thus there could be the single leader or there could be multiple leaders of different parties or groups. And a culture either permits the one or welcomes the many. Culture, in other words, provides the environment for leadership continuity and for leadership change.

The third subject that we discussed could come under the general heading of changes of leaders or leadership change. I find that the points made by the different speakers were as follows: the rise and fall of leaders do not imply that political and religious and military leaders are necessarily in harmony, that is that they all fall and all rise at the same time; rather that they can be seen very often as independently rising or falling. Thus a religious leader may be continuous while a political leader contemporary with him declines. Leaders do not fall all at once within any particular culture. Secondly, the tactics of leaders are conditioned by the culture and the institutions. The point was made that generalizations about any tactics in different cultures have to be made with the greatest and most careful discriminations. There are certain historical moments, however, especially those of crisis, that seem highly encouraging to the rise of leaders, particularly political leaders. Again, the diverse aims of different leaders characterize a democratic society. It is precisely because there are competing leaders in a democratic society that we have the tensions and divisions in such a society. A leadership crisis in an authoritarian society, however, results not from participation but from preventing participation of followers in the possession and transfer of power.

And the final heading under which I list my education in this seminar is the relation of ideology to leadership. The point was made repeatedly that leaders claim for their programs rational values regardless whether they possess such values. They make claims for their programs that are rational and that will best serve their followers, even though such claims may never be fulfilled. Indeed, Bailey argued that leaders are identified by their capacity to persuade others to follow them, regardless of the validity of their claims. Again leaders identify their goals with single interests or with communal interests (or with heavenly interests), but always leaders are identified as establishing clear and clearly announced goals. And the final point in regard to leadership and ideology was that the leader's rhetoric constitutes the means by which he imposes his ideology on his followers.

THOMPSON: I shall comment on just one question: should we study leadership? We ought to examine that question with the same rigor that our two visitors have examined both their agreements and differences. And we ought to think about at least three issues that become problems when one looks at leadership. The first of these is our ambivalence about leadership. The second is our uncertainty about the nature of leadership. And the third is our dimly perceived concept of future leadership or the demands of the future with regard to leadership.

Our ambivalence regarding leadership seems to be rooted essentially in our ambivalence about power. We have said much less about power in this conference than would a group of political scientists meeting alone. That is unfortunate, because we might deepen our understanding of this phenomenon if we were to draw on the several insights that a group of this kind has to bring to bear on this question. Our ambivalence, I think, stems from the fact that on the one hand we see the exercise of power as absolutely essential to organized efforts and to solutions of problems. And yet both for ourselves and for others we see the use of power as somehow morally inferior and offensive to our sense of what we ought to be and what the world requires of us. In the entourage discussion we were a little bit uneasy when we lowered the sights of our discussion to the practical questions of politics. Within any organization one tends to find one of two attitudes toward the exercise of power. One is illustrated by a colleague who was recently given an assignment at this university: he believed that if he did not seize power in the management of the small areas of responsibility in the first few weeks of office, he would have no role to play whatsoever. As a result he began assuming responsibility for tasks formally exercised by a committee. He was so explicit and so instantaneous in his notion about the sole way of achieving something organizationally that he perhaps lost the opportunity in the long run to strengthen this important area of activity within the university. The opposite view is the view many of us take: we complain about what happens in our department, in our state, in the world, but really leave the task essentially to others. I find it much easier to say what I think ought to happen in the government department than to make a serious contribution in the inevitable planning, organizing, implementing of certain important choices. To steer one's way between these two extremes seems to me important. The only reassurance one might offer people within our particular context, which is not necessarily the context of kings and rulers, is that power in most social institutions in America is transitory. Leadership is something one performs for a while and then turns over to others. And that ought to be, in some way, a corrective to the either the great desire to have power or the fear of use of power and the avoidance of it.

The second thing is our uncertainty about the nature of power. When Andrew Cordier was named President of Columbia University following a number of distinguished intellectuals, everybody laughed. Here was a rather overweight, retired United Nations diplomat who had performed a useful role after the student rebellions at Columbia because he simply sat and listened, and according to a colleague, he out-listened and out-sat all his adversaries. Somehow he compensated for whatever lack of vision and vaulting educational ideas he had by his persistent resolute attention to each problem as it came along. He did a better job in a crisis situation than his predecessor had done in that respect. Our uncertainty about leadership, it seems to me, is born of the fact that leadership is a curious blend of vision. And any leader, on the other hand, has to move back and forth between some set of concepts and principles, goals and dreams that he may have, and the hard, grubby task of giving them form and shape. Somehow the leader must accept the fact that there are stubborn realities, moral realities, for example, that may require harsh decisions very often as well as gentle and supportive decisions. But the leader must also deal with the drudgery of his office. And drudgery it seems to me is a vital and crucial aspect of leadership if leadership is to be any more than symbolic.

The final area which is the most serious of all is leadership for the future. This brings us into the very heart and center of the discussion. We are tempted in thinking about leadership in the future to throw overboard all that we may have learned and all that may have been written and said about leadership in the past. I was struck with the fact that Professor Roth, having said the balance of power is probably irrelevant to our current problems, immediately mentioned that Europe ought to throw its weight into the balance to bring the United States and the Soviet Union to the negotiating table. The management of a crisis, the accommodation of conflicting interests, the discovery of convergent interests can be accomplished, if they can be accomplished at all, only by those who try to make use of those techniques which a leader was perhaps least able to bring to bear on his particular rulership in an earlier period. One reason that no attention to other forms of leadership, to the models of art and history and literature, relevant is that these may be frail wreaths as we think about how to bring men together and how to avoid their pulling too far apart.

But these models happen to be the only wreaths we have. They happen to be, even in such an area as the historian of interest to several of us Herbert Butterfield has announced, even in such an area as taking a risk for peace. Butterfield, who happened to be a religious historian, argued that he supported Kissinger, not as a person who is always ready to give away everything, but as a hard-headed Bismarkian diplomat. The West ought to be prepared, he said, to take a chance for peace in terms of some new venture. Julian Hartt was asking us, it seemed to me, to at least think about the fact that we might have to innovate in whatever measures were employed. Leadership for the future, therefore, would require both some drawing upon the wisdom of the past and some willingness to try something new if one had reasonable hope that that might lead to a resolution. My colleagues would much prefer to study the relationship between the agencies of government, the various aspects of the White House, and the White House and the cabinet than to study leadership in general. There is in a specialized age in this world a mounting suspicion that when one talks about leadership one may be talking about everything in general and nothing in particular. But if one could dispose of this suspicion and dispose of these three other issues that I have mentioned, leadership in general could be one of the most worthwhile and valuable areas for continued inquiry.

THORUP: In relation to the leadership for future: In the West the unprecedented destructiveness of nuclear weapons has produced the conviction that these weapons have no rational application in an offensive mode. In the Soviet Union, by contrast, this very same destructive quality makes nuclear weapons the decisive weapons of modern warfare. Institutes in the Soviet Union which publish information on warfare were cited as support for this comparison. In this situation the peace movement may impair the political capacity of the West to act, whereas the East need not experience such a disadvantage. We have just seen an example of the rise of a movement in Poland which in essence threatened the political structure and we have seen what happened to that movement as a result. We find no balance between West and East, because the lack of tolerance for leadership expressed in the West is denied expression in the Soviet Union or its satellites. This imbalance puts the West in a way at a disadvantage, but at the same time it puts us in closer touch with the people who express such frustration. To that extent leadership becomes more opaque for the individual the further he or she gets from where the decisions are being made.

I would like to see this group study leadership in relation to the prospect of nuclear war. As Roth pointed out, there is no leadership in the peace movement, there is no focus for survival. There is no one place that I can see that talks about survival. The United Nations is so splintered because no country is willing to relinquish its own sovereignty to achieve a higher level of cooperation. Somehow we have got to transcend that state of affairs. If one has any doubt that a common focus for survival is essential, the physicians for nuclear responsibility have demonstrated very effectively that there is no way the medical profession can help in a nuclear war. None. There is no way that people damaged and injured in a nuclear war are going to be helped by modern medicine. When one thinks about the destruction of all medical facilities and the vast majority of all medical personnel (since they are mostly located in the cities), one imagines chaos. There will be no hope of survival for those people that are left. And it will be a constant destruction of those people as radiation takes it toll. And unless we can overcome this one thing, there is no future. I think it becomes the prime concern of all. Maybe we can in the course of discussion look for a way to address this concern. But some dramatic move has got to be undertaken. The majority of people here in this country think that there is going to be a nuclear exchange. How in the world can we get to this point without trying to do something to avert this horrible prospect?

THOMPSON: Regarding a possible presentation at the United Nations: the near misses for diplomatic success in this area would be an illuminating topic for scholars to explore. Dean Rusk recalled that on the very eve that Johnson planned to go to Moscow the Soviet invasion of Czechoslavakia occurred. The very moment when there was to have been arms negotiations, invasion of Afghanistan took place. Cambodia bombing. If one reads the history of the inter-war period, he is struck by how many accidental factors moved history one way or another. There was always a left regime in Germany when there was a right regime in France. Thus historians writing about the period talk about how different it might have been if the constellations had been different. But it might be worth somebody looking at the forks in the road which almost lead in a somewhat different direction than our present situation. And that a group like this could likely carry out.

KHARE: This is the time for a vote of thanks to all the participants in the conference. The organizers remain grateful to the guests from the West Coast and to those from within the University, and of course to all the members of the Committee for making the conference an intellectually rewarding experience.

Appendix

APPENDIX

Committee on Comparative Study of Individual and Society

The Committee on Comparative Study of Individual and Society, sponsored by the Center for Advanced Studies of the University of Virginia, offers an intellectual forum to scholars drawn from different departments and schools of the University.

Objectives

The broad objective of the Committee is to facilitate and foster a free exchange of scholarly information across different disciplines and specializations. Its focus on the individual's relationship to wider society reflects a vital dimension of the Jeffersonian heritage of the University of Virginia. The Committee encourages original and creative scholarship on the enduring issues of cultural values, science and technology, and historical change. Its concerns are comparative, humane and global. Programs of the Committee generally encourage links between the theoretical and practical problems, and the immediate and ultimate concerns.

Organization

The Committee is composed of scholars representing different disciplines at the University. The executive and planning affairs of the Committee are handled by the Chairman of the Committee, who is appointed by the Director of the Center for Advanced Studies for a term of three years. Members of the Committee are also appointed for a similar term by the Director at the advice of the Chairman. He also brings together the Committee members for planning and conducting specific projects.

The Committee was informally assembled in the Spring of 1974 and formalized in 1977. It encourages interdisciplinary collaboration in research, graduate teaching, and public programs. It offers opportunities for scholarly exchange through informal talks, research seminars, public lectures, occasional conferences, and the biennial Virginia Lectures. It occasionally invites scholars from within the United States and abroad to give the Virginia Lectures and to participate in specific seminars. These guests enrich the intellectual life by becoming available to other segments of the University. Taking its mandate broadly, the issues discussed so far have included individual privacy, autonomy, and dignity in technological societies; individual in law and medicine; leadership in Western and non-Western societies; historical change in art and culture; science, technology, and social ethics; bureaucracy and social values; the changing work ethic; and human global survival.

Programs

The major programs of the Committee include the following:

Virginia Lectures on Individual and Society - These lectures are held biennially since the Fall, 1977. The lecturers so far have been Professor Rodney Needham (University of Oxford), Professor John Holloway (University of Cambridge), and Professor Jeffreie Murphy (University of Arizona). Professor Needham's lectures were published by the University Press of Virginia as a book, Primordial Characters.

Spring Semester Panel Discussion - Every Spring the Committee invites a reputable scholar to make a presentation of general interest before the University audience. The presentation is usually followed by a panel discussion, reflecting the interdisciplinary interests of the Committee. The following scholars have appeared on this program: Professors Milton Singer (University of Chicago); Mary Douglas (Russell Sage Foundation); Robert Livingston (University of California School of Medicine, San Diego); Alasdair MacIntyre (Boston University); and Philip Abelson (Editor, Science, American Association for Advancement of Science).

Occasional lectures - The Committee also invites occasionally scholars from within the University and outside to give lectures on a topic of their choice. These are arranged according to the convenience of the particular scholar. Those who have spoken in this forum include Professor M. N. Srinivas (Cornell University; Institute for Social and Economic Change, Bangalore, India); Professor Victor Turner (University of Virginia); Dr. Thomas Murphy (Director, Federal Executive Institute, Charlottesville).

Conferences - Occasionally conferences are organized by the Committee. A three-day conference on Leadership was held in March, 1982 at the Birdwood Pavilion of the University of Virginia. Besides the members of the Committee, two external scholars were invited: Professor Guenther Roth (University of Washington), and Professor F. G. Bailey (University of California, San Diego). The proceedings of such conferences are usually published.

Monthly talks - Members of the Committee utilize this (informal and formal) forum during the academic session for presenting a talk on their current research. The meetings are open to all interested members of the University faculty and students.

Other Programs - The other programs that this Committee has undertaken in the past include seminars and forums on "the bureaucrat as a person," "privacy issues and public record, "secrecy and Freedom of Information Act," and "professional and personal ethics among the administrators." These seminars were held in collaboration with the Federal Executive Institute, Charlottesville, Virginia.

MEMBERSHIP

Caplow, Theodore
Department of Sociology
542 Cabell Hall
University of Virginia
Charlottesville, VA   22903

Childress, James
Department of Religious
    Studies
102 Cocke Hall
University of Virginia
Charlottesville, VA   22903

Claude, Inis L., Jr.
Government and Foreign Affairs
207 Cabell Hall
University of Virginia
Charlottesville, VA   22903

Cohen, Ralph
Department of English
234 Wilson Hall
University of Virginia
Charlottesville, VA   22903

Germino, Dante
Government and Foreign
    Affairs
203 Cabell Hall
University of Virginia
Charlottesville, VA   22903

Hartt, Julian
Kenan Professor of Religious
    Studies Emeritus
1939 Thomson Road
Charlottesville, VA   22901

Howard, AE Dick
Law School 359A
University of Virginia
Charlottesville, VA   22903

Khare, R. S. (Chairman of
    Committee)
Department of Anthropology
303 Brooks Hall
University of Virginia
Charlottesville, VA   22903

Langbaum, David
Department of English
Wilson Hall
University of Virginia
Charlottesville, VA   22903

Little, David
Department of Religious
    Studies
B106 Cocke Hall
University of Virginia
Charlottesville, VA   22903

Noble, Julian
Department of Physics
Beams Lab 312
University of Virginia
Charlottesville, VA   22903

Rorty, Richard
Department of English
Wilson Hall
University of Virginia
Charlottesville, VA   22903

Appendix

Shannon, David
Department of History
210 Randall Hall
University of Virginia
Charlottesville, VA   22903

Simmons, Alan
Department of Philosophy
506 Cabell Hall
University of Virginia
Charlottesville, VA   22903

Thompson, Kenneth
Government and Foreign Affairs
232 Cabell Hall
University of Virginia
Charlottesville, VA   22903

Thorup, Oscar A., Jr.
Associate Dean, Medical School
School of Medicine 1074
University of Virginia
Charlottesville, VA   22903

Trefil, James S.
Department of Physics
Beams Lab 322
University of Virginia
Charlottesville, VA   22903